D1716515

JOAN OF ARC

Warrior Saint of France

PAUL B. THOMPSON

Enslow Publishers, Inc.
40 Industrial Road
Box 398
Berkeley Heights, NJ 07922
USA

http://www.enslow.com

Library of Congress Cataloging-in-Publication Data

Thompson, Paul B.
    Joan of Arc : warrior saint of France / Paul B. Thompson.
        p. cm. — (Rulers of the Middle Ages)
    Includes bibliographical references and index.
    ISBN-13: 978-0-7660-2716-9
    ISBN-10: 0-7660-2716-3
    1. Joan, of Arc, Saint, 1412-1431—Juvenile literature. 2. Christian women saints—France—
Biography—Juvenile literature. 3. France—History—Charles VII, 1422-1461—Juvenile literature.
I. Title.
    DC103.5.T56 2006
    944'.026092—dc22
    [B]

                                         2006034061

To Our Readers:
We have done our best to make sure all Internet Addresses in this book were active and
appropriate when we went to press. However, the author and the publisher have no control over
and assume no liability for the material available on those Internet sites or on other Web sites they
may link to. Any comments or suggestions can be sent by e-mail to comments@enslow.com or to
the address on the back cover.

Illustration Credits: The Art Archive/Dagli Orti, p. 53; Bibliotheque Nationale, Paris,
France/Bridgeman Art Library, p. 85; © Corel Corporation, p. 127; Enslow Publishers, Inc.,
pp. 12, 21, 35; Erich Lessing/Art Resource, NY, pp. 38, 64, 116–117; Mathias Gabel, pp. 29, 42;
Original painting by Corey Wolfe, p. 4; Réunion des Musées Nationaux/Art Resource, NY,
pp. 56, 110; Wikipedia.org, p. 75.

Illustration Used in Design: Reproduced from *Full-Color Picture Sourcebook of Historic
Ornament,* published by Dover Publications, Inc.

Cover Illustration: Original Painting by Corey Wolfe

CONTENTS

FATE OR BETRAYAL?

COMPIÈGNE WAS UNDER SIEGE. OUTSIDE THE
city's walls, soldiers of the duchy of Burgundy kept close
watch, making sure no supplies or reinforcements entered
the French town. It was May 24, 1430, the ninety-third
year of the Hundred Years War between England and
France.

Burgundy, a wealthy and populous province in eastern
France, was allied with England. For many years the dukes
of Burgundy fought the kings of France over who would
rule the country. War, assassination, and intrigue were the
order of the day. Duke Philip of Burgundy, known as Philip
the Good, bore a long-standing grudge against King
Charles VII of France, who was thought to have had a hand
in the assassination of Philip's father, John the Fearless, in
1419.[1] Philip the Good also wanted to add as much of
Charles's territory to his own realm as he could seize. His
alliance with England was a means to that end.

Between 1415 and 1430, Compiègne had been attacked no less than eight times by English or Burgundian troops. It had been occupied by the French, the Burgundians, and the English in turn.[2] Taking heart from French victories of 1429 in the Loire valley, the people of Compiègne rebelled against their English garrison and drove them out. Triumphant, they sent the keys to the city to the recently crowned King Charles VII, pledging their loyalty to him. This was not just a symbolic gesture, as when dignitaries receive oversized ceremonial keys nowadays. In 1429, the keys to a city were exactly that— they unlocked the main gates, allowing full access to the town. Compiègne was placing its fate in the hands of Charles VII, trusting him to defend them against further attacks.[3]

Late in the day on May 24, 1430, the drawbridge on one of the fortified gates of Compiègne clattered down. Five hundred French soldiers emerged, determined to drive the Burgundians away from the city and lift the siege. They were an odd assortment: adventure-seeking nobles, hard-bitten mercenaries, and patriots who yearned to see France free of foreign occupation. Most remarkable of all was their leader, the eighteen-year-old daughter of a sheep farmer from Lorraine—Joan of Arc.

In an age when women had little power, few legal rights, and no social standing apart from their male relatives, Joan of Arc had inspired the dejected French to rise up and fight the invaders of their land with new confidence. Guided by inner voices she claimed were Saint Margaret, Saint Catherine, and the archangel Michael, she

WHAT WAS HER NAME?

In English-speaking countries, she is known as Joan of Arc. This is a direct translation of her later French name, Jeanne d'Arc. But who or what is "Arc?" A place? A family name?

Her parents were Jacques Darc and Isabelle Romée. In various documents, the family name is also spelled Dart, Dars (the final *s* is silent in French), Darx, Tard, and even Tart.[4] People of common birth seldom knew how to write their own names, and the scribes who did the writing for them spelled the names as they heard them.

The nobility of Europe used a different system of naming. Men and women of noble birth had a Christian name they were given at birth. Their family name was derived from the place name where they were from. For instance, the English regent in Joan's time was John of Lancaster. John of Lancaster was better known by his title, the Duke of Bedford.

In French, *de* means "of," as in Duc de Bourbon. If the *de* precedes a word starting with a vowel, the *e* is replaced with an apostrophe (Duc d'Alençon). By this example, one might think Joan was of noble birth—Jeanne d'Arc—but she wasn't. During her lifetime, no one ever called her Jeanne d'Arc. At her trial, she called herself Jehanne la Pucelle, meaning Joan the Maiden. Court records refer to her as Jehanne or Jeanne Darc. As her fame grew to match her deeds, her name grew too, transforming Jehanne Darc, a peasant girl, into the noble-sounding Jeanne d'Arc.

To make matters more confusing, King Charles VII ennobled Joan's family as a reward for her services to him. He granted them the name Du Lys, meaning "of the Lily," a reference to the lilies on his own coat of arms. Joan's descendants through her surviving brothers bore the name Du Lys for centuries after.

led by example, standing in the thick of battle bearing the banner of her God and king. She lived the hard life of a soldier and was wounded in combat more than once. She did all this while wearing men's clothes and armor, though she never tried to disguise her true gender.

As the leader of a great patriotic movement, Joan of Arc lived by a strict moral code and required her followers to do the same. Always referring to herself as "la Pucelle" (the Maiden), Joan gathered loyal followers from every rank of French society. Dukes, counts, and barons willingly enrolled in her cause, as did thousands of ordinary Frenchmen. The peasant girl from Domrémy astonished everyone by winning victory after victory against the formerly invincible English. In May and June 1429, fighting at Orléans, Meung-sur-Loire, Beaugency, and Patay, Joan's army cleared the Loire valley of invaders.

With success came fame, and soon her name alone was enough to spread terror among the English. While Joan of Arc's followers believed she was sent by God to save France, the English could only attribute their sudden reversal of fortune to sorcery. They claimed Joan the Maiden must be a witch.[5]

Joan arrived at Compiègne on May 13, 1430. The town fathers welcomed her with open arms. She brought with her two thousand men eager to defend the city. The commander of Compiègne's garrison, Guillaume de Flavy, was respectful but aloof. Like many professional soldiers serving the king of France, he regarded the young Joan as a dangerous asset at best.[6] Her common origins did not sit well with many aristocrats, including several close advisers to Charles VII. They found Joan useful when fighting the English, but if her leadership led other peasants to take up arms to right perceived wrongs, the whole of France might be engulfed in revolution.[7,8]

True to her fiery nature, Joan decided the best way to defend Compiègne was to attack a nearby English stronghold. Her military successes were often due to the fact that she struck at unusual times and places, taking her enemies by surprise.

At dawn on May 15, Joan's army crept out of Compiègne to strike the English. For the first time, her inspirational presence and unusual tactics did not bring victory. The English army proved much stronger than she had suspected, and the French were driven back into the city.

Rebuffed but determined, Joan decided to attack where the English and Burgundian armies joined, through the towns of Ourscamp, Sempigny, and Noyon, and drive them apart.[9] With the enemy armies separated, each could be defeated in turn. Joan led her soldiers to Soissons. She hoped to cross a key bridge there to begin her campaign to divide the invaders, but a strange thing happened. The commander of French forces in Soissons, Guichard Bournel, would not let Joan or her army into the city. They had to camp outside. The reason for this rejection soon became clear. Bournel had made a treacherous deal with the enemy. For four thousand pieces of gold, Bournel betrayed his king and delivered Soissons to John of Luxembourg, a follower of Duke Philip of Burgundy.[10]

In a moment, Joan's fortunes changed radically. From a promising offensive against the English and Burgundians, she now found herself surrounded in enemy territory. She had no choice but to retreat again to Compiègne. The situation there had grown worse as well. While her army was camped outside Soissons, the Duke of Burgundy had thrown a temporary bridge across the Oise River and sent his army across to lay siege to Compiègne. Joan reached the city safely on May 22, evading the Burgundians along the way.

The stage was now set for the battle on the evening of May 24, 1430. With just five hundred soldiers (including her brother Pierre), Joan left the city for a fortified gatehouse on the opposite bank of the river. From there she planned to raid the English camp, using the growing darkness to disguise her purpose and numbers. Her bad luck continued. Instead of a camp full of unsuspecting English soldiers, she ran into an alert company of Burgundians who greatly outnumbered her. The French fought hard, but they had no chance to break through. Joan ordered a hasty retreat to the gatehouse. She stayed behind, rallying her men, trying to gain time for the rest of her band to reach safety. To the French soldiers' horror, they found the drawbridge to the gatehouse had been raised. They were locked out, marooned outside the defenses of Compiègne and surrounded by the enemy.

Who was responsible for this shocking turn? Everyone agreed it was the order of Guillaume de Flavy, military commander of Compiègne. De Flavy claimed later that it was necessary to raise the drawbridge behind Joan to prevent the Burgundians breaking through and seizing the gatehouse. From there they could cross the 450-foot Oise River bridge and attack Compiègne directly. De Flavy's excuse did not persuade many. The defenses on the city side of the bridge were strong and well-manned. The city walls were lined with artillery, and the garrison had been alerted by Joan's battle on the riverbank. To many, de Flavy's abandonment of Joan was treachery.[11]

Cries of treason went up from the men, so recently betrayed at Soissons. Still fighting valiantly, the last of Joan's men, led by Joan herself, were overwhelmed. The Burgundians knew full well whom they were fighting. Joan carried a distinctive banner into battle, a great flag bearing the lilies of France, an image of Christ on the throne of Heaven, and the motto Jhesus-Maria.[12] The Burgundians made every effort to take Joan alive. An archer named Lyonnel, part of the company commanded by Lionel of Wandomme, dragged Joan from the saddle and subdued her.[13]

That ended the fight. The most famous warrior in France, the savior of Orléans, and the girl who made Charles VII king was in the hands of her enemies.

The Burgundians had captured Joan of Arc.

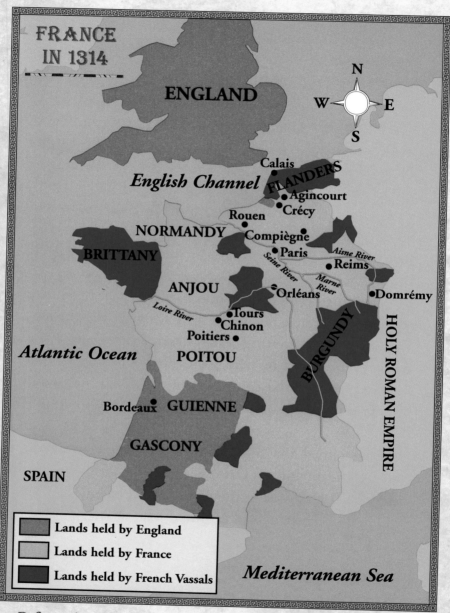

FRANCE IN 1314

ENGLAND

N
W — E
S

Calais

English Channel

FLANDERS

Agincourt

Crécy

Rouen

NORMANDY

Compiègne

Paris

Aisne River

BRITTANY

Seine River

Reims

Marne River

ANJOU

Orléans

Domrémy

Loire River

Tours

Chinon

Poitiers

BURGUNDY

HOLY ROMAN EMPIRE

Atlantic Ocean

POITOU

Bordeaux

GUIENNE

GASCONY

SPAIN

Mediterranean Sea

Lands held by England

Lands held by France

Lands held by French Vassals

Before the Hundred Years War, the English ruled over a section of Southern France and an even smaller portion in the north. While the French king owned most of France, French vassals had also carved out their own possessions.

THE HUNDRED YEARS WAR

THE HUNDRED YEARS WAR BETWEEN ENGLAND and France actually lasted 115 years. Three things that would ignite the war were the nation-building ambitions of the French monarchy; England's attempt to keep the parts of France that had once belonged to their king, Henry II; and the desire of the province of Flanders (in present-day Belgium) to free itself from the repressive grip of France.

Origins

King Edward II of England's wife, Isabella, was the sister of three kings of France: Louis X, Philip V, and Charles IV. She was a strong woman who tired of her husband's inept rule and raised an army against him. Supported by the great barons of England, Isabella overthrew Edward II in 1327 in favor of their son, soon to be Edward III. The deposed king was murdered eight months later.

13

All this time, the French king, Philip VI, plotted against England's French holdings south of the Loire. Alarmed, Edward III tried to collect allies against France, but his effort resulted in little real support. Then a crisis in Flanders brought everything to a head.

England and Flanders had long enjoyed a trade partnership. English wool was shipped to Flanders, where it was woven into cloth. Trade with Flanders made English wool growers rich. Flemish weavers also reaped handsome rewards from their trade in cloth.

The Flemings had often been unhappy under French authority, which was repressive. Taxes drained the Flemings' wealth, enriching their enemy and England's, the king of France. By 1325, the weavers had formed their own ruling council, the Commune, and deposed the Count of Flanders. Philip VI was not about to lose such a valuable province. He sent an army to take the province back. In 1328, the French destroyed the Flemish militia at Cassel. The French army occupied Flanders and harshly reasserted control.

In response to the invasion of Flanders, Edward III placed an embargo on wool exports. This hurt his own people and the Flemings as much as it cost Philip VI in taxes. Some weavers from Ghent, suffering from both the French occupation and the English embargo, made a pact with Edward III in 1338. The Flemings' goal was enough to ensure English aid against another French invasion, but the Flemish leader, van Artevelde, also urged Edward III to claim the throne of France for himself.

He had a case. Edward III was the grandson of Philip IV of France. Philip's daughter, Isabella, was wife and queen to Edward II.

Philip IV had three sons, all of whom ruled in turn because none of them had a male heir. When the last, Charles IV, died in 1328, he was succeeded by his cousin, Philip VI. Philip VI was the son of King Philip IV's brother Charles, Count of Valois. When Charles IV died without an heir in 1328, the dynasty founded by Hugh Capet in A.D. 987 came to an end. Thereafter, the line of kings descended from Philip VI became known as the House of Valois.

In most cases, a grandson had precedence over a nephew in matters of succession. To deny Edward's claim, the French invoked the Salic Law, which stated that royal succession could only happen through male heirs, not female. As Edward III descended from Philip IV through his daughter, Isabella, he was barred from claiming the throne of France. Whether or not the Salic Law had any standing in France was another matter, but no one much cared. The House of Valois had the throne of France and they were not giving it up.

War was openly declared in 1338. Philip VI claimed all of Edward's French lands and invaded Guienne to prove it. Edward III gathered his army and landed in Flanders to challenge the French.

ENGLISH VERSUS FRENCH

England's prospects in the war did not look good. France was larger, richer, and more heavily populated. By summoning his great nobles, Philip VI of France could field a large army of armored knights. The French king could tax anyone in his realm with a stroke of a pen. Edward III had to contend with political opposition at home, and he needed the permission of Parliament to raise money for his campaigns.

Edward, however, had several important advantages the French did not recognize. His army was tough and experienced, coming off recent wars in Scotland. What Edward III lacked in numbers of knights he more than made up for in tactics and firepower, for his army was equipped with a corps of longbowmen.

Edward III's first victory came at sea. On June 24, 1340, an English fleet bearing soldiers to the continent encountered a French fleet in the port of Sluys. A bloody battle ensued, and the French fleet was destroyed. Estimates of French losses ran as high as eighteen thousand in this one battle.

THE BATTLE OF CRÉCY

In 1346, Edward III landed a new army in Normandy. He marched inland, burning towns and laying waste to the countryside. Angrily, the great nobles of France demanded King Philip stop the invaders. Philip VI gathered an army of thirty-five thousand to confront Edward. Only 1,141 of

THE LONGBOW

In the thirteenth century, the English had learned about the longbow when it was used against them by the Welsh. The longbow was about six feet long unstrung. It could hurl a "cloth-yard shaft" up to three hundred yards. (Arrows were called "cloth-yard shafts" because they were the same length as a yard of cloth.) An experienced longbowman could shoot five or six aimed arrows a minute and as many as twelve a minute in unaimed volleys.

Edward's army usually took the field with five to ten thousand archers, backed by a few thousand foot soldiers and cavalry. The hail of arrows the longbowmen could hurl was devastating. Word of what the longbow could do must have reached France, but the French nobility believed the armored knight on horseback was master of the battlefield. The way they saw it, they were not afraid of commoners with oversized bows.

Edward's 10,000 men were knights. The rest were foot soldiers and longbowmen. The armies met near the village of Crécy on August 26, 1346.

Outnumbered, Edward III protected his flanks with obstacles, the River Maye on one end and the houses of the village of Wadicourt on the other. He drew up his infantry in two large blocks, and in between them posted his longbowmen. His position was on rising ground. The archers set up sharpened stakes and dug holes in the turf to ward off French horsemen.

Philip's army arrived, strung out along the road. Seeing the English defenses, he sent a company of crossbowmen from Genoa to bombard the English. Crossbows were deadly, but their best rate of fire was three arrows per minute. A longbow could double that with precise, aimed fire, and quadruple that rate in volleys. The Genoese fell back, unable to compete with the longbowmen. Seeing their withdrawal, the French knights called them cowards and trampled the retreating Genoese.

The French spotted the English nobles in the center of the line and crowded together to reach them. The longbowmen had them under fire a full three minutes before the French even reached the English position. Five thousand longbowmen could put fifty thousand arrows into the air each minute. In three minutes, the French came under a deluge of one hundred-fifty thousand arrows. The French horses were cut down by this deadly hail. The greatest knights in France toppled into the mud, where they were easily slain by English foot soldiers.

The appalling slaughter went on. Fifteen times the French charged, and every attack was broken by a storm of arrows. More than ten thousand French knights, lords, and princes died at Crécy. English losses were very small. Philip's broken army streamed away, leaving Edward III master of the battlefield.

THE BLACK PRINCE

Philip VI was succeeded by his son, John II, in 1350. Brave and courtly, John was the wrong man for the job. He spent money frivolously, ruining the kingdom's finances. In 1355, he faced invasion on three fronts: a seaborne attack on Brittany, a landing across the English Channel, and another landing near the city of Bordeaux. The last expedition was led by Edward III's son, Edward, Prince of Wales. Known as the Black Prince from his habit of wearing armor of that color, Prince Edward had fought at Crécy when he was just sixteen years old. Now twenty-six, he was every bit the general his father was.

John II gathered another large army of knights and moved to meet the Black Prince. They met at Poitiers on September 19, 1356. Again the English anchored their position with obstacles on either flank. Lacking natural ones, they dug trenches to fend off the French cavalry.

The French had decided their defeat at Crécy came about because their horses were shot out from under them. Therefore, they reasoned, they would attack the English on foot. Their greater numbers and superior valor could not fail to carry the day.

The weather was hot. French knights, including King John, dismounted their horses and marched stolidly toward the English line. They had half a mile of open ground to cover, and arrows began to fall on them, eighty thousand before they reached Prince Edward. They did reach the English knights, but they were so exhausted and weakened by arrows they were easy prey when the Black Prince remounted his knights and charged. Two thousand French nobles were taken prisoner, including King John II. Thousands more were slain on the long, blazing retreat.

The consequences of Poitiers were enormous. Royal authority in France reached its lowest ebb in a thousand years. Chaos reigned in many districts. Laws were broken, taxes went unpaid, and the discredited French aristocracy had to fight to keep their own homes and land safe.

To remedy the collapse of authority, the ancient assembly known as the Estates-General had to be called in 1357 to reorganize the machinery of government. Made up of representatives of the Catholic Church, the aristocracy, and the wealthy commoners, the Estates-General passed a law to regulate the collection and dispersal of taxes in France. Unfortunately, the assembly fell prey to internal bickering and made bad political decisions, quickly alienating the people it was meant to serve. The failure of the Estates-General immediately led to a peasant revolt known as the *Jacquerie*. Weary of their homeland being plundered and bled dry by heavy taxation, French peasants attacked government officials, burned manor houses, and murdered churchmen and nobles.

John II's eighteen year-old son Charles ruled France while his father was captive in England. Charles raised loyal companies of troops and suppressed the Jacquerie with the same savagery his forebears used against the rebellious Flemings. With this success in hand, Charles felt strong enough to reject the treaty his father made with England. John II had signed away all the territories once ruled by Henry II in the twelfth century and won back, bit by bit, by the kings of France since.

England was almost as exhausted as France. It had won great victories but lacked the money and manpower to

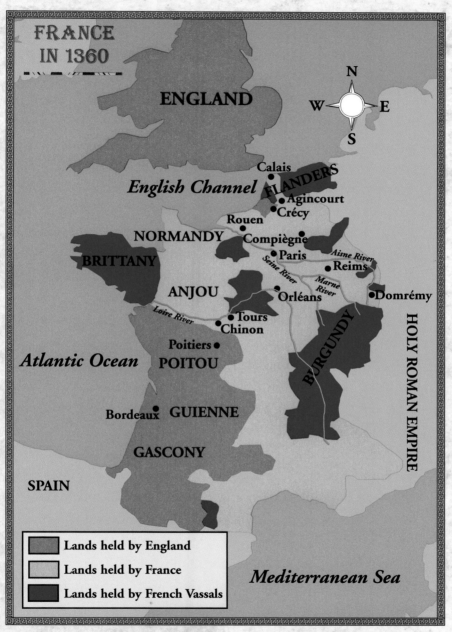

FRANCE IN 1360

ENGLAND

N
W   E
S

English Channel

Calais
FLANDERS
Agincourt
Crécy

Rouen

NORMANDY

Compiègne

BRITTANY

Paris

Aisne River

Seine River

Reims

ANJOU

Marne River

Orléans

Domrémy

Loire River

Tours
Chinon

BURGUNDY

Atlantic Ocean

Poitiers

POITOU

HOLY ROMAN EMPIRE

Bordeaux

GUIENNE

GASCONY

SPAIN

Mediterranean Sea

Lands held by England

Lands held by France

Lands held by French Vassals

By 1360, the English and their French vassal allies had expanded their control over French lands.

hold onto vast stretches of French territory. When Prince Charles rejected the treaty his captive father made, Edward had no choice but to accept a simple armistice in 1360 called the Peace of Bretigny. Edward III dropped (but did not renounce) his claim to the French throne. In return, Prince Charles yielded land all over France: Guienne in the southwest, Calais in the northeast, and Ponthieu. He promised to pay a huge ransom for his father, John II. Charles made a down payment on the ransom, and the King was released, leaving a number of hostages in England in his stead until the ransom was paid in full. John II was not very popular when he returned home. His drastic failure at Poitiers and the burden of his enormous ransom did not endear him to his subjects. It was widely known he had a comfortable, even luxurious stay in England. When one of John's hostages escaped, honor required him to return to England to serve out his captivity. He died a pampered prisoner in 1364. His son became King Charles V.

Again a change of ruler signaled a major change in a nation's fortunes. Charles V was no warrior, but he was an able ruler. Saddled with the Estates-General, he whittled away its power and privileges until it became little more than a debating society. Charles resumed tax collection, rebuilt fortresses, and tried to establish a full-time, professional army in place of the old mob of headstrong knights and nobles.

One of Charles V's best choices was to appoint Bertrand du Guesclin Constable of France (commander of the royal army). Open war resumed in 1369, and du

Guesclin was ready. To frustrate the English, du Guesclin adopted tactics to counter the superior might of the English army. He avoided open battle with Edward III or the Black Prince. He besieged castles held by the English, or built new ones to command important locations. He ambushed small bands of English troops with a highly trained force of his own choosing. By these methods du Guesclin undid the losses of Poitiers and Crécy. By 1372 the Constable of France had reconquered Brittany and Poitou.

After many campaigns, the Black Prince died in 1376. He was forty-five years old. His father, King Edward III, survived his son by one year. For the next thirty years, England was wracked by a struggle between two rival family lines, Lancaster and York. The Lancastrians gained the upper hand in 1399 when Edward III's son Richard II was deposed and a man of their line, Henry Bolingbroke, assumed the throne as Henry IV.

ARMAGNACS VERSUS BURGUNDIANS

France also had a new king in 1380. Charles VI was too young to rule, so a regency was created by his powerful uncles, the dukes of Anjou, Berry, and Burgundy. The dukes ruled in the boy king's stead, and their policies rapidly brought the country to ruin. France's economy collapsed again, while taxes remained heavy and repression even heavier. The regent dukes cared little about ordinary Frenchmen, and they ran the government to enrich themselves.

After the Duke of Anjou died in 1384, Philip, Duke of Burgundy became virtual dictator of France. Charles VI tried to assert his own power by dismissing Philip and appointing his brother Louis, Duke of Orléans, in his place. Charles VI's attempts to bring order only caused more chaos. The Duke of Burgundy formed an opposition party to the Duke of Orléans, beginning a split in French politics that would almost destroy the country. In addition, Charles VI developed periodic bouts of insanity starting in 1396. These would continue for the rest of his long, unhappy life.

In 1404, the new Duke of Burgundy, John the Fearless, arranged the murder of the Duke of Orléans. The assassination was quite popular in some parts of France—in Paris, for example, where Orléans and his policies were hated—but it led to open conflict between the two factions. Leadership of the Orléans party fell to the father-in-law of the new duke of Orléans, the Count d'Armagnac. Thereafter, the two sides were known as the Armagnacs and the Burgundians, and their bitter feud progressed to open warfare.

The differences between the Armagnacs and Burgundians came down to this: Followers of the Duke of Burgundy favored peace with England, even at the cost of French territory. The Armagnacs wanted to fight on and recover all occupied French land. Burgundy's support was strongest in the northeast and in the city of Paris. The Armagnac faction's base was the heartland of France, in the Loire River valley.

A New Invasion

Against this fractured nation England's new king, Henry V, launched an invasion of Normandy in 1415. He had just 10,000 men, half of whom were longbowmen. Charles VI summoned his lords to battle, and 30,000 knights responded to the sovereign's call. Henry V fell back, having lost a third of his men to sickness and battle. At Agincourt, on October 25, 1415, the two nations clashed once more.

Henry had barely six thousand effective soldiers that day, including five thousand archers. He drew his men up in the now classic formation, with his flanks secured by thick woods on either side. The open ground narrowed, so that anyone riding toward the English would find the room to maneuver progressively shrinking.

The French army, led by a new Constable of France (the Duke of Armagnac, no less) showed it had learned nothing from Crécy, Poitiers, or the campaigns of Bertrand du Guesclin. They crowded in, shoulder to shoulder, to charge the few English men-at-arms around King Henry. The ground was muddy, and the first two lines of French dismounted so as not to be shot off their horses by the longbowmen. They tramped a quarter of a mile in armor under a heavy arrow barrage. The field narrowed, forcing the French knights in tighter and tighter. They reached the English and by sheer weight of numbers pushed them back. As they did, they came under short-range, aimed fire from longbowmen on both flanks. The first French attack bogged down in a welter of mud and blood. Into this shambles the second line doggedly marched, only adding to the confusion and slaughter. The third line, still mounted, saw the writing on the wall and shamefully rode away, abandoning their comrades to their fate.

Forty-six hundred French knights and men-at-arms perished at Agincourt, along with uncounted thousands of common infantry. Reports of English losses vary; they do not seem to have been more than a few hundred.

Normandy fell to Henry in short order, and Charles VI had to make peace. His rival, the Duke of Burgundy, negotiated the Treaty of Troyes in 1420. In it, Henry V was given Charles VI's daughter Catherine as his queen, and the king of France had to adopt Henry V as his son and heir. The true French heir, the Dauphin Charles, was summarily declared illegitimate. The pro-peace faction, including the University of Paris, the Estates-General, and the Burgundians, approved this surprising change.

The Dauphin, as the crown prince of France was called, refused to accept the treaty. He fought on until his forces were driven beyond the Loire. He made his headquarters in the city of Bourges. Bereft of money, soldiers, and luck, the Dauphin seemed a spent force. He was derisively called *le petit Roi de Bourges*, the little King of Bourges.

Poor, haunted Charles VI died in 1422. Henry V was supposed to succeed him as King of France, but misfortune claimed the valiant young king's life the same year.

In 1422, the English occupied half of France's territory, and much of what remained was loyal to the Duke of Burgundy, an enemy of Dauphin Charles.

FROM DOMRÉMY TO DAUPHIN

THERE WAS NOTHING REMARKABLE ABOUT THE village of Domrémy. It was like a hundred other villages in the province of Lorraine or like thousands throughout France. The inhabitants were peasants who worked small farms or tended flocks of cattle or sheep. The placid Meuse River flows through the valley where Domrémy lies. In the fifteenth century, much of the land around the village was wooded. Wolves and bears were still common in the deeper recesses of the forest.

For years, soldiers of Burgundy, England, and those serving the crown of France had marched and counter-marched across Lorraine. It made little difference to the peasants which side occupied them. Soldiers robbed, raped, and murdered with impunity, as they did anywhere war displaced peace. For the powerless people of Domrémy, there was no comfort but religion. A well-known shrine, Notre Dame de Bermont, was a few miles from the village. It was a popular site for local pilgrimages.

27

Another popular spot near Domrémy was the Bois Chenu, the Ancient Woods. It was widely believed that fairies lived among the dark oaks.[1] In medieval Europe, people did not believe fairies to be tiny winged creatures, like Tinkerbell in *Peter Pan*, but human-sized beings with magical powers. Country folk believed they were an elder race, created in the twilight time before mortal men entered the world. Having magical powers put the fairies in an ambiguous position with the Church. They were not demons, but neither were they children of God. To believe in them was natural. To consort with them was dangerous.

Joan of Arc was born in Domrémy, probably in 1412. She did not know the exact date of her birth (peasants who could not read or write had no way of recording such events) and only later was the date of January 6 fixed as her birthday.[2] The date is more symbolic than historical. January 6 is Epiphany, or Twelfth Night, the day the Magi are said to have visited the infant Christ in Bethlehem. There is no record of Joan's true birthday, but it's celebrated on January 6, and the date has become traditional.

Her father was Jacques Darc, a farmer and man of some substance in the village. He owned land and served as an elected official in Domrémy for many years. His relatively well-to-do situation reflected the change in peasants' status since the Black Death, an epidemic of a disease called the bubonic plague, in 1348.[3] With farm labor and landowners alike reduced by one third, labor became a valuable resource. Enterprising peasants could command higher wages, which they used to enlarge their

Joan of Arc's childhood home is a tourist site today. It has been carefully maintained and converted to a museum for the public.

holdings and add moneymaking enterprises, like livestock breeding, to their basic farming income.

Jacques's wife was Isabelle Romée. Romée was not her surname but a title given to those who had completed a pilgrimage to Rome.[4]

Joan was the Darcs' second daughter and their fourth child. She was a serious, quiet girl, devoted to her family and her Catholic faith. Neighbors recalled years later that Joan was a likable girl but too serious to be a good playmate. She spent a lot of time at church and seldom missed a service unless her duties tending the Darcs' herd of sheep kept her away. Her mother was her chief teacher in matters of religion.[5] Joan learned all the usual skills of a country girl of that age—spinning wool and weaving cloth, sewing, and cooking. Less traditional but more useful in her later life was her skill riding a horse that she learned plowing her father's field.[6]

Joan's life in Domrémy was normal for her time and place. She joined in some local festivities, such as when she and other children danced around an ancient tree in the Bois Chenu known as the Fairy Tree.[7] They entwined the tree with garlands of flowers and danced around it, singing. Joan thought little of it at the time or later. It was something the children of Domrémy did, a pastime, like skipping stones on the river.

There was no question about young Joan's virtue. Her father had stern ideas on that score, vowing he would drown Joan himself if she strayed from a righteous path.[8] He did not have to worry. With great dedication for a girl so young, Joan's early life was vigorous and virtuous. She worked daily in the pasture, tending the family flock, and avoided the usual distractions of youth. When she misbehaved, it was for a higher cause. She was known to play hooky from work on saints' days to walk to the next village to worship at the shrine of Notre Dame de Bermont.[9] Despite the conditions in war-torn Lorraine, she managed to make this trip many times on foot without difficulty. Sometimes a brother or friend would accompany her, but Joan was not afraid to go alone. Soldiers were constantly about, but she managed to avoid being robbed or molested.

Joan had no schooling. She never learned to read, and only near the end of her life did she learn to write a single word—her name. Despite this handicap, she was clear-thinking and expressive, and when the situation called for it, she was capable of forceful eloquence.

As often happens with famous people of the past, there has been a great deal of speculation about Joan's appearance. Because she was such a popular subject for French artists down to the present day, there are as many different representations of Joan as there are portraits. Conventional pictures of the late Middle Ages show a romantic image of Joan, with long golden hair, a slender frame, and blue eyes. Even when depicted in armor, she is more damsel than warrior.

Only one drawing was made of her during her life, a doodle made by a Parisian clerk in the margin of a letter reporting the battle of Orléans. Little more than a cartoon, it shows a young girl with a high forehead, long, wavy hair, and a prominent nose.[10] There's no evidence the clerk ever saw Joan, but it shows how curious people were about her appearance even during her lifetime.

It was admitted by her enemies as well as her friends that Joan of Arc lived and died a virgin. This was a vital part of her reputation. Joan's power to inspire the fighting men of France derived in part from her purity, her deep religious convictions, and her claim to have received numerous messages from angels and saints. To the medieval mind, only a virtuous woman, a virgin like the Mother of Christ, was worthy to receive divine revelations. This is why her enemies tried to blacken Joan's reputation by implying she was the lover of any number of high French leaders. None of these insults stuck. During her life, she submitted to more than one physical examination to confirm her virginity.

So what did Joan of Arc look like? None of her contemporaries sang the praises of her beauty. A few observers have given us glimpses of the real girl. Her physique has been described as sturdy. This makes sense. Joan was a farm girl, and she probably worked every day of her life. Life made her rugged and strong. During her military adventures, her stamina became legendary. She outlasted many veteran soldiers on long marches, and she bore the wounds she received in combat without complaint.

Her hair was probably black. A strand of black hair, enclosed with a letter signed with her name (Joan would have had someone write the letter for her), was preserved for many years in the town of Riom.[11] (It has since been lost.) Given the physical characteristics of the people living in the Meuse valley then and now, her eyes were likely dark as well. The image that emerges of Joan is as a hardy, honest girl, with an uncommonly strong will and keen moral sense.

VOICES AT NOON

In 1425, at age twelve or thirteen, Joan heard her voices for the first time. It was noon on a summer day, and she was in her father's garden working when she heard a male voice and saw a great light. Frightened, she knew it was "a worthy voice . . . sent by God."[12] The voice's first message to her was a simple admonition for Joan to go to church and be as good a person as she could be. Joan's response was to swear to remain a virgin until God or his angels directed her to marry.

After her third encounter with the male voice, Joan decided she was hearing an angel. Before long, she saw the being that addressed her, saw him as plainly as she saw anyone. Only much later did she identify him as the angel Saint Michael, whose image she had no doubt seen before.

Saint Michael's advice about proper living was soon followed by admonitions of a different sort. He told Joan she must "go to France." Though Domrémy was part of France, the unworldly Joan understood that the angel meant she should go to the heart of France, west of her home province.[13] France was where the king dwelled, and for a peasant girl this meant the land ruled by God's anointed monarch.

When Joan asked why she should go to France, Saint Michael told her France was in a state of great misery. He then said she would receive visitations from two saints, Saint Catherine and Saint Margaret. Joan must listen to them and do as they bid. After Saint Michael vanished, Joan kissed the ground where he had stood.[14]

Before long, the women saints visited Joan. They appeared crowned, and they spoke to the young girl in beautiful, clear voices. (Thereafter, Joan refused to describe her visions in detail. She knew skeptics would question her about the supposed appearance of the saints, and she did not want to muddy the message of her voices by getting bogged down in details of costume or figure.)

The voices and visitations came more regularly, almost daily, for three years. By 1428, their orders were more exact and persistent: Joan must go to France and save the nation. England and Burgundy held France in a tight grip and were slowly strangling it. Dauphin Charles, still uncrowned at age twenty-two, lived at the castle of Chinon, surrounded by greedy and inept councillors. The war continued, as captains loyal to France (if not to Dauphin Charles) fought the hated English and Burgundians as best they could.

JOAN STARTS HER MISSION

Convinced by the power and beauty of her visions, Joan resolved to obey her saints. The voices did not require her to keep her mission secret, but Joan feared word of her quest would reach the Burgundians, who were never far away from her village. She therefore went directly to the nearest commander of royalist troops, Robert de Baudricourt.[15] De Baudricourt was in Vaucouleurs, a town about ten miles north of Domrémy. Joan told her story to de Baudricourt, who was not impressed at first. After listening to Joan, he told one of his men to "take her back to the house of her father and . . . give her a smacking."[16]

Joan said to him, "The kingdom of France is not the dauphin's but my Lord's. But my Lord wills that the dauphin shall be made king and have the kingdom in custody."[17] De Baudricourt asked who her Lord was.

Joan replied, "The King of Heaven."

De Baudricourt laughed at this sixteen-year-old-peasant girl who claimed to be on a mission from God to save France. He dismissed her with a few coarse remarks.

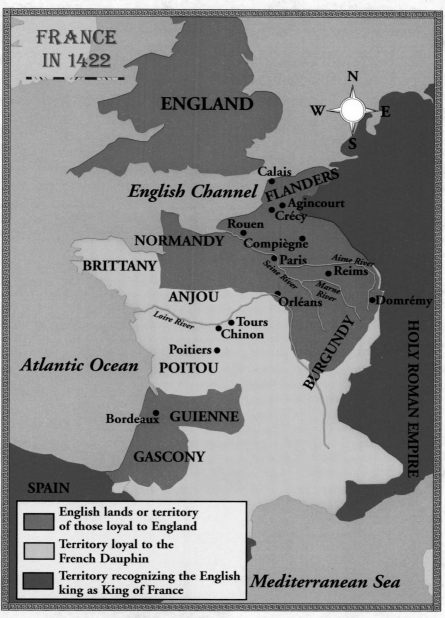

FRANCE IN 1422

ENGLAND

N
W · E
S

Calais
English Channel FLANDERS
Agincourt
Crécy
Rouen
NORMANDY Compiègne
BRITTANY Paris
Aisne River
Seine River Reims
ANJOU Marne River
Loire River Orléans Domrémy
Tours
Chinon
Poitiers BURGUNDY
Atlantic Ocean POITOU HOLY ROMAN EMPIRE

Bordeaux GUIENNE

GASCONY

SPAIN

English lands or territory of those loyal to England
Territory loyal to the French Dauphin
Territory recognizing the English king as King of France

Mediterranean Sea

Most of the cities and villages important to the Hundred Years War and the quest of Joan of Arc were located in northern France, which was controlled by England.

Joan went home, but the voices would not let her rest. She left Domrémy for the last time and returned to Vaucouleurs in January 1429. By then, the town was under threat from a Burgundian army, and de Baudricourt was more willing to enlist any help he could get. Joan repeated her message from her voices that she could save France. She urged de Baudricourt to send her to the embattled city of Orléans, which the English were besieging. There she swore she would turn the tide against the invaders.

As no one else was doing much to save the country, de Baudricourt decided to pass her along to the dauphin. Joan left Vaucouleurs February 23 with an armed escort. Baudricourt said to her as she rode past, "Come what may."[18] Not a ringing endorsement, but Robert de Baudricourt was the first of many French soldiers to hear Joan's charismatic message. Not all soldiers were impressed with her right away. It is said de Baudricourt's soldiers escorting Joan considered abandoning her along the road because they thought she was crazy. The more time they spent with her, however, the more the rough warriors came to respect her and, in time, venerate her.[19]

In Vaucouleurs, Joan donned men's clothing. At first it may have been a ploy to disguise her (rumors of a mystical maiden from Lorraine were spreading), but Joan readily accepted her new clothes with her new role. This was not a casual change for her to make. Wearing the clothing of the opposite sex was not only considered strange, it was a crime. However, Joan was not afraid of any mortal law, not while her voices were with her.

More than three hundred miles separated Vaucouleurs from Chinon, no small journey in those days. Word of Joan's coming preceded her. At Chinon, Dauphin Charles's advisers debated whether or not he should see the strange girl from Lorraine. She might be insane, or her message might be a trick of the Burgundians. If the dauphin granted her an interview, it might be seen abroad as a measure of his desperation or a mark of gullibility. Nevertheless, Charles's advisers did not try to turn Joan away. She arrived at Chinon on March 6, 1429.[20]

The man Joan was so driven to see was not a gallant warrior like his predecessor, King John II, or a calm, calculating schemer like Charles V. The dauphin was physically weak and unattractive. He had thin arms, spindly legs, a bulbous nose, small gray eyes, and a large round head. He was lazy and inclined to whine about his misfortunes rather than keep a kingly stiff upper lip. Charles was extravagant with his friends and tightfisted with everyone else. He was poor. It was said he borrowed money from everyone, even his cook. He wanted to be handsome, noble, and popular, and he was not. What Charles did possess, though few recognized it in 1429, was an ability to pick capable underlings and get the best performance out of them. For this he was later known as Charles the Well-Served.[21]

Joan's entrance into the dauphin's court has been dramatized many times in plays, films, and novels. It must have been a striking scene. The peasant girl from Domrémy, naïve and uncouth, entered a hall filled with great lords and ladies of France. Joan had cut her hair short, like a

Joan's arrival at the Castle of Chinon is depicted in this fifteenth century German tapestry, which is in the Centre Jeanne d'Arc in Orleans, France.

man, and wore a black tunic. For days, she had lingered outside, unable to enter without the dauphin's permission. They exchanged letters about why she had come. (Joan dictated her replies.) The dauphin interviewed the men of her escort about her and their trip. The soldiers gave glowing accounts of Joan's piety and virtue and told how they had miraculously evaded all danger to reach Chinon.

Curious to meet this prodigy, Charles summoned Joan to the castle. He dressed drably and mixed among the members of his court. It was dark, and the torch-lit hall was crowded with three hundred people. Despite this,

Joan went directly to Charles, curtsied, and said, "Gentle Dauphin, I am called Joan the Maiden. The King of Heaven sends me to you with the message that you shall be anointed and crowned in the city of Reims, and that you shall be the lieutenant of the King of Heaven, who is the King of France."[22]

Still Charles tried to fool her. He pointed to one of his vassals nearby and told her he was the dauphin. She was not deceived and called him noble prince. Her faultless identification of the dauphin caused quite a stir and won Charles's further attention. Taking the strange girl aside for a private word, Charles received personal proof of Joan's supernatural connections. She asked him if she could tell him something only he knew, as proof that her voices were real and her mission genuine. Charles agreed.

According to later accounts, Joan told him that on November 1 of the previous year the dauphin had been praying by himself in the chapel of the castle of Loches. He asked God for three things: to end the war if Charles was not the true heir to the throne of France; that he, the dauphin, be punished if his resistance to the English was causing suffering among innocent people; and that the sins of all his subjects be forgiven.[23]

Stunned, Charles admitted Joan was right. No one else knew about his three requests of God, not even his confessor. When he and the girl from Domrémy returned to the waiting court, a profound change in the dauphin's manner was noted. In one momentous meeting, Joan had won the confidence of the prince.

ORLÉANS

JOAN SPENT THREE DAYS AT CHINON AS THE prince's honored guest. She attended mass daily and conversed with churchmen attached to the dauphin's court. More importantly, she befriended John II, Duke d'Alençon.

The twenty-two-year-old duke was one of the dauphin's staunchest supporters. Duke d'Alençon had been fighting the English since he was seventeen. Captured at the battle of Verneuil in 1424, d'Alençon had to pay an enormous ransom to regain his freedom. Raising money for the ransom cost him his land and titles, and d'Alençon's wife was forced to pawn her jewels.[1] His hatred for the English can be imagined.

D'Alençon was out hunting when Joan arrived at Chinon. When he heard about the peasant girl who had so impressed the dauphin, he hurried to the castle to meet her. When d'Alençon was introduced, Joan said boldly, "You are very welcome! The more men of the blood royal of France that are gathered together, the better."[2] The Duke d'Alençon would become Joan's greatest supporter, surpassing the dauphin in his constant faith in Joan and her mission. She ever after referred to him as *mon beau duc*, "my fair duke."[3]

Impressed as Dauphin Charles was, he was not about to hand over his army to a teenage peasant girl. Her visions had to be explored by experienced clergymen, to make certain they were not delusions or heresy. Joan was packed off to the University of Poitiers on March 11, 1429. The learned churchmen questioned her for eleven days. A transcript of Joan's examination was made, but it has since been lost. She emerged unscathed, weathering complex and dangerous theological questions with unusual skill for one so young and unschooled. When she was asked for a sign that would prove the truth of her claims, she replied, "I am not come to Poitiers to make signs. But lead me to Orléans; I will show signs to you for which I was sent."[4]

Joan won over her judges completely. They sent her back to the dauphin, who had one other test to make. In the city of Tours, Joan submitted to a physical examination (conducted by the dauphin's mother-in-law, the queen of Sicily) intended to prove her virginity. It was a vital part of Joan's story that she be a virtuous woman. If she were not, it would call into question everything else she had said and done. She passed this test too.

With this double confirmation, the dauphin at last agreed to send Joan to Orléans with an army to raise the siege of the city. While the army was being organized, Joan

Pictured are the remains of the hall where Joan first met the Dauphin Charles.

obeyed a new instruction from her voices and made a battle standard for her men.

It was a large sheet of white canvas, fringed with silk on a field of fleur-de-lis (lilies, the symbol of the French monarchy). In the center was painted an image of Jesus holding the world in his hand, or possibly more fleur-de-lis. On either side of Christ was an angel, with the motto *Jhesus Maria* (Jesus and Mary) written alongside. Joan would ride at the head of Dauphin Charles's army bearing her banner to inform the world of her mission to save France.

An immigrant Scottish painter in Tours named Hamish Power made the banner. It cost the dauphin twenty-five pounds. Power actually made two standards for Joan, one large, one small. The famous one was the larger of the two. The smaller pennant was the standard of

Joan's personal company of soldiers. It depicted a dove with a scroll in its beak with the words *De par le Roy du Ciel* (On behalf of the King of Heaven).

The dauphin also contributed a practical gift: He had a suit of armor made for Joan. It was what soldiers of the day called a full harness, that is, a complete suit of armor, made to fit Joan alone.

She received her armor prior to May 10, 1429. On that day, the dauphin paid his master armorer one hundred pounds for a "complete harness," that is, a suit of armor for Joan. By 1420, European armor was almost exclusively made of articulated steel plates, carefully molded to the wearer's shape. Judging from accounts of Joan's vigor in battle, she had no difficulty climbing, running, and leading troops in her armor.

Her armor protected her during battle, but Joan never used her sword or any other weapon. Shouting encouragement, she led her men into the fray, carrying just her flag. At her trial, she declared she liked her standard "forty times" better than her sword. Questioned about her equipment at her trial, Joan of Arc replied unequivocally: "I bore this standard when we went forward against the enemy to avoid killing anyone. I have never killed anyone."[5]

She obtained a sword in a very dramatic way. Robert de Baudricourt had given her a blade when she left Vaucoleurs; but while in Tours or Chinon, Joan received new information from her voices and acted on it. She sent one of her men to the monastery of St.-Catherine-de-Fierbois to dig around the altar for a sword she was told lay hidden there. (As a female, she could not enter a monastery.) To the surprise of the monks, the man found a fine steel weapon buried below the altar. Cleaned up, the sword proved to have five crosses engraved on the blade. It was probably a crusader's weapon, left in the monastery when the owner took holy orders years before. Finding it gave Joan's reputation as a wonder worker another boost.[6]

JOAN'S ARMY EMBARKS

Word of la Pucelle and her mission drew recruits to Chinon. The army to relieve Orléans swelled to a sizable force, between ten thousand and twelve thousand men. When the army left Chinon in May 1429, everyone was in high spirits. The royalist Armagnac forces had long been bereft of hope. Joan had already achieved one great victory by getting the army together and sent on its way.

Their destination, Orléans, was the key to the Loire River region. In 1428, the English under the command of the Earl of Salisbury invaded the Loire in an attempt to cut off the dauphin from his loyal lands farther east. Had the English succeeded in taking Orléans, eastern France would have been easy pickings for their Burgundian allies.

Salisbury undertook the invasion with a paltry force of five thousand men. At first, he was successful, capturing seven lesser towns while his army was reduced to little more than three thousand soldiers. Faced with the walls of Orléans, Salisbury simply did not have the manpower to surround so large a city. Fifteen hundred Burgundians reinforced him, but this hardly helped.[7] Unable to encircle the city, Salisbury did the next best thing: He built a series of log forts along the roads serving Orléans, cutting off all traffic. He sent his men to patrol between the forts to cut off any French who tried to slip in or out of the city. The blockade was tight, but not perfect. Messengers got out of Orléans with some regularity, and small parties of soldiers made their way in.

With or without Joan, a competently led French army should have been able to force its way through Salisbury's thin lines and relieve the city. It is a measure of how demoralized the French were by 1429 that a large town like Orléans could be threatened by so small an enemy army.

The key to Orléans was a single fortified gate, called the Tourelles. It guarded a span of bridge that was the only way across the Loire River. Salisbury made the Tourelles his prime target, and once he began attacking it, the French abandoned the gate and withdrew across the river, breaking down the stone bridge behind them. A short time later, the capable Earl of Salisbury, a general with long experience campaigning in France, was killed when a cannonball struck him as he stood in a window of the Tourelles studying the defenses of Orléans.[8]

The loss of the Earl of Salisbury greatly weakened the English-Burgundian army. There was no one of similar skill to replace him. Attacks on the city petered out, and the remaining English troops dug themselves in, constructing more fortifications to hold out against expected French counterattacks. Long before Joan and her army arrived, the English had surrendered initiative to the French.

The people of Orléans resisted valiantly despite bombardment by English cannons. On some occasions, armed citizens sallied forth to attack the besiegers without the knowledge or support of the French soldiers in the city.

Commanding troops in the city were two stalwart leaders. In overall command was John, Count of Dunois, the illegitimate son of Louis, Duke of Orléans.[9] He was also the dauphin's cousin. John of Dunois had a distinguished record fighting the English, but at Orléans he seemed baffled by the enemy's imposing fortifications. Before Joan arrived, he advocated evacuating the city and letting it fall to the English.[10]

With John of Dunois was a famous captain, Étienne de Vignolles, known to all as La Hire, "the Hothead." La Hire had spent his entire adult life fighting the English. A bold, violent man, he led his company of veteran soldiers to Orléans in October 1428 to help defend the city. In between fending off attacks by Salisbury's men, La Hire journeyed to Chinon to argue for more aid to the beleaguered city. It is not clear whether he was at Chinon when Joan arrived or if he met her at Orléans, but regardless of when he met the Maid, La Hire became one of her most famous companions. She even managed to convince him to moderate his infamously profane language.[11]

On February 12, John of Dunois led a large French force to intercept an English convoy of food and supplies for the besiegers at Orléans. The English made a stand in an open field, drawing their supply wagons around them like castle walls. When the French soldiers arrived, they outnumbered the English ten to one. They opened the battle by blasting the wagon circle with cannon from beyond the range at which English longbows could reply. Cannon fire did great damage to the English, and if the French had persisted, they might have destroyed them. Pride and pointless valor took hold of the French nobles, however, and they launched a cavalry attack on the wagons. The English longbowmen went into action, decimating the mounted attack. While the French milled around outside the circle of wagons, English troops came out and drove them off. What began as a certain victory ended in another rout due to the French nobles lack of discipline.[12]

French knights fought for personal glory and honor. Individual feats of bravery were valued far more than military efficiency. French knights preferred to capture noble opponents for ransom rather than kill them. Against lowborn enemies, like the Flemish militia, they could be ruthless. For daring to take up arms against noblemen, the Flemings deserved only death.

The English longbowman was neither knight nor noble. He was a freeborn subject of his king who took professional pride in his fighting skills. Without romantic notions of chivalry, the English soldier did his duty and fought to win. He would kill any enemy in his path, whether he was king, count, or commoner.

The English convoy carried many barrels of salted fish to feed the army at Orléans. During the cannonade, barrels were smashed apart, scattering fish everywhere. Thereafter the fight was known as the Battle of the Herrings.

Joan sent a letter to the English after she left Poitiers. Here are some excerpts:

> King of England, and you, Duke of Bedford, you call yourself regent of France, you William de la Pole, Sir John Talbot, and you Sir Thomas Scales . . . go back to your own countries, for God's sake. And if you do not do so, wait for the word of the Maid, who will come visit you briefly, to your great damage . . . [those who do not] do not obey, I shall have them all killed. And if they wish to obey, I shall have mercy on them. . . . You shall never hold the kingdom of France from God, the King of Heaven, the son of St. Mary; but King Charles, the true heir, will hold it.[13]

There was more—admonishing the great lords of England to obey a French farm girl, cease fighting, and go home.

It is tempting to think of this letter, the first of several Joan would dictate during her career, as an attempt to undermine English morale and raise the spirits of the people of Orléans. In truth, the letter was exactly what it purported to be: a warning to the English that God's instrument, Joan the Maid, was coming to drive them out of France. The English now had fair warning. If they stayed, whatever fate befell them was their own fault for defying God.

Arrival at Blois

On April 21, 1429, Joan arrived at Blois with her army. John of Dunois went to meet her. Like Robert de Baudricourt, he was not impressed at first. He may have resented the airs of this peasant girl who claimed to be coming to do the job he had failed to do—save Orléans—but once he saw the army she led, he changed his mind.

On April 26, Joan's army left Blois for Orléans. Avoiding towns occupied by the English, the French reached the city three days later. Joan's first act was to try to send boatloads of food across the river to Orléans, but a contrary wind prevented them from going. Annoyed by the delay, she announced she would go into the city. What happened next was considered a miracle. The winds changed immediately. Supply boats and Joan the Maid sailed across the Loire to the city.

Joan's arrival was only a temporary solution to Orléans' problem. The large train of supplies trailing back through the countryside could not be loaded on boats. The siege would have to be broken in order for the vital supplies to enter Orléans. The first obstacle for Joan was a potent English fort at St. Loup. She led her army right past the enemy position, with the supply train behind. The English let them pass unmolested. This was also called a miracle, but what actually happened was a large band of French soldiers and townsmen came out of Orléans to attack St. Loup. Joan and her people passed in safety because the small English garrison had its hands full holding off a furious diversion.[14]

Joan's arrival at the head of an army, along with a bounty of food and medicine, buoyed the spirits of Orléans. The Maid was not so pleased. She wanted to attack the English and break the siege at once. When French commanders did not arrange an attack the next day, she grew angry again. Despite her appointment by the dauphin, she could not give orders to men like La Hire or John of Dunois. They outranked her, they were soldiers, and they were men.

Fuming, Joan went to one of the forward French positions, facing the English-held Tourelles just a few yards away. Shouting across the broken bridge, she told them to obey God and surrender. The English soldiers replied with obscenities.[15]

Later, when the English illegally held a French herald captive, she sent word to them that she would have all English prisoners in Orléans executed if the herald was not released. The English relented, but with the freed messenger they sent a threat: If Joan fell into their hands, they would "torture and burn her, and that she was nothing but a rustic, and that she should return to herding her cattle."[16]

John of Dunois left the city on May 1 to confer with other French commanders at Blois. While he was gone, Joan acted. On May 2, she inspected each English fort while staying well out of bowshot. She spent the night in the church of Ste. Croix in Orléans, communing with her voices.

John of Dunois returned as news reached Joan that an English army under Sir John Fastolf was on its way to reinforce the Orléans besiegers. When confronted by Joan, John of Dunois admitted he knew about the approaching English army. Outraged, Joan told him if Fastolf got through she would cut his (John of Dunois) head off.[17]

Why not attack the besiegers before help arrived, Joan demanded? The French commander was unwilling, believing the English forts were too strong to assault. Joan knew better, having looked them over while John of Dunois was away, but she couldn't challenge him anymore. Dismayed at her commander's timidity, she went to bed.

Joan had hardly gone to sleep before one of her voices told her to go at once and attack the English. She awoke immediately, calling her followers to arms. On May 4, they stormed the fort at St. Loup, a small but sturdy outpost manned by tough professional soldiers. The fight lasted three hours and ended when every Englishman in St. Loup lay dead. A relief force was sent to help the garrison, but Joan's men drove them off, killing 140 and capturing 40 more.[18]

It was her first battle, and she had handled herself well. Joan was in the thick of the fighting, leading her men on with her great banner. While her courage was great, she was only seventeen and not used to such violence. When the battle was over, Joan wept at the sight of slain English soldiers.[19] John of Dunois, who might have punished Joan for violating his orders, recognized her success and forgave her impetuous attack.

The next day, Joan sent another letter to the English, again ordering them out of France. It was, she said, their third and final warning. It was ignored.

After losing St. Loup, the English abandoned their fort at St. Jean le Blanc, which coincidentally had been Joan's next target. To keep the English off balance, she led her buoyant followers in a fierce assault on the fort facing the

Tourelles, a former Augustin convent. A French officer, Lord Gaucourt, tried to stop this attack, but Joan, La Hire, and her excited soldiers brushed him aside and stormed the English bastion. The Maid was at the forefront of the close, brutal battle, and it left her exhausted.[20]

The English position was now very perilous. Their most powerful fort, the stone gate of the Tourelles, was trapped between the river and the newly captured Augustin convent. Cannon were dragged to the convent and trained on the gates of the Tourelles. Once again John of Dunois and other lords tried to hold Joan back. Since the city had been restocked with food, it was wiser, they said, to wait until the dauphin could send an army to free them. Joan had grown used to her commanders' opinions, and she shrugged off the nobles' advice, saying she had better advice from God. Later that night, she told her companion Jean Pasquerel she expected to be wounded the next day.[21]

On May 7, 1429, a Saturday, the French attacked the Tourelles early in the morning, and an intense, bloody battle ensued. Cannon fired at point-blank range, and much close fighting was done with sword, ax, and mace. The English garrison was seven hundred strong, the largest group left in the besiegers' army. They drove the French back time and again, and at one point, an arrow hit Joan. Striking between her neck and shoulder, the arrow made a wound six inches deep, but the valiant Maid remained in the fight, refusing help or medical aid.

The battle raged until eight o'clock in the evening. John of Dunois wanted to end the attack, as the French had many casualties and it was growing dark. Joan asked him to wait a little while longer. Bleeding from her wound, she took her banner and led an exhausted band of soldiers up scaling ladders to the rampart of the fort. Seeing the Maid coming on despite her wound, backed by scores of shouting followers, English resistance collapsed. A few surrendered, while others tried to escape. Some leaped from the gate into the river, but their heavy armor dragged them down. Among them was William Glasdale, the English commander of the Tourelles, who had obscenely mocked Joan's surrender demands.[22]

Though other English forts still remained west of the city, the fall of the Tourelles spelled the end of the siege of Orléans. The bridge behind the gatehouse was hastily repaired, and Joan rode triumphantly into the city. Crowds cheered, church bells rang, and hymns were sung. Then the Maid and her army went back to the blood-soaked Tourelles to defend it in case the English tried to take it back. They never did.

On May 8, the remaining English troops filed out of

Joan entered Orléans in triumph.

their forts and drew up in battle formation. A large force of French soldiers came out of Orléans to oppose them. It was Sunday, and Joan forbade her men to launch any attack on the Lord's Day. If attacked, they could defend themselves as fiercely as they liked, but they were not to go after the depleted English.

The bait untaken, the English could do nothing. Their great victories of Crécy, Poitiers, Agincourt, even the Battle of the Herrings, were all made from defensive positions. When Joan refused to attack them, they could do nothing but withdraw. Their numbers were too small to assault the French. Joan let them go. By applying her faith, the Maid had defeated the English army's greatest tactic.

Winning the Loire

NEWS OF THE RELIEF OF ORLÉANS CAUSED celebrations in France and alarm among the English and their allies. Dauphin Charles composed an open letter to his subjects after Orléans was saved, describing the successive overthrow of the English at St. Loup, the Augustin convent, and the Tourelles. (It was on the Paris copy of Charles's letter that the clerk copying it, Clement de Fauquembergue, drew his famous doodle of how he thought Joan must look.).

Oddly, the dauphin did not mention Joan's part in the victory at all in this letter.[1] Later historians have pondered why he did this. Was Charles being discreet, protecting Joan in her unusual role as spiritual leader of the army? Joan wearing men's clothing and bearing arms was contrary to many laws—was the dauphin trying to shield the Maid from gossip and persecution? Or was Charles already thinking ahead to the time when he did not need the valiant peasant girl?

The only known drawing of Joan was made on a copy of one of Dauphin Charles's letters in the records of the Paris Parliament.

Whatever the dauphin's motives, he failed to keep Joan out of the limelight. Within a very short time, all of France (indeed, all of Europe) knew about the peasant girl who broke the siege of Orléans. To many, Joan was the heroine of the age. She was compared to Hannibal, Alexander the Great, and Julius Caesar as a military leader.[2] Others were intrigued by tales of her voices. The ill, the unlucky, and those yearning for spiritual fulfillment wrote to Joan, begging for advice, a cure, or an audience. The Duchess of Milan even invited Joan to take command of her realm.[3]

Joan declined these offers. Her mission in France was not done; it was just beginning. Her next task was to see the dauphin crowned king in the city of Reims, traditional site for the coronation of the kings of France.

The sensation caused by Orléans inspired poets and mythmakers across Europe. In Italy and in English-held Paris, tracts were written about the miraculous details of Joan's early life. It was said roosters crowed on the night she was born. Some wrote that while tending her father's sheep, birds alighted on her shoulders, and wild animals came to her when she called. Other accounts claimed that Joan rode and fought for six straight days in full armor without tiring. When confronted by the profane Sir William Glasdale, English commander of the Tourelles, Joan prophesied his death by "without bleeding,"[4] and so on. None of these tales were true, but they achieved wide circulation, and many have stuck to Joan as "facts" to this day.

The English reaction to Joan and Orléans was not so colorful. The overall commander of English forces in France and regent for the underage King Henry VI, the Duke of Bedford, wrote a letter home as well. In it he complained:

> There fell, by the hand of God, as it seemeth, a great stroke upon your people that was assembled there [at Orléans] in great number, caused in great part, as I trow [believe], of sad belief and unlawful doubt that they had of a disciple and limb of the Fiend [i.e., Satan], called the Pucelle, that used false enchantments and sorcery.[5]

Already the English claim that Joan was a witch and a satanic impostor had surfaced. The belief would grow stronger in coming days.

Defeated at Orléans, the English army retreated to Meung. The French let them go. In a reversal of their roles at Orléans, the commanders wanted to pursue the beaten foe, and it was Joan who held them back. She realized the beaten English army would spread word of their defeat more effectively than any royal letter.

Joan left Orléans to confer with the dauphin. Charles had moved to Tours, and there the two met on May 10, 1429.[6] Charles praised her before his delighted court, but Joan was not about to be deflected from her mission by flattery. She urged Charles to go with her to Reims and be crowned at once. He was reluctant. Reims was in enemy territory. The route there was thick with English and Burgundian soldiers. Better to continue the campaign in the Loire valley, liberating captured towns and driving the English into Normandy. Prompted by his councillors, Charles asked Joan what her voices told her to do.

"Go," they said. Go to Reims? "Go and I will help thee," said the voices.[7]

She needed help. French casualties at Orléans had been heavy; several hundred at least lost out of an army of no more than two thousand.[8] The official commanders of the dauphin's army, the Duke d'Alençon and John of Dunois, met with Charles and Joan at Loches to obtain the dauphin's permission to raise more troops. The call went out, and the ranks of Joan's army swelled again.

It was still a modest force. When Joan marched on the city of Jargeau, she had twelve hundred knights, plus comparable numbers of infantry, archers, and cannoneers. At the same time, Sir John Fastolf's English army left Paris for the Loire. The usually adept Sir John proceeded with great caution, even though his army of four thousand outnumbered Joan's.[9] There was a new confidence among the French because of the victory at Orléans. Sir John surely knew this, and it affected his thinking. His march south was so slow he had no part in the opening of the Loire valley campaign, and he only participated at the end.

THE BATTLE OF JARGEAU

The Duke d'Alençon was in formal command when the struggle to free the Loire began in June 1429, but Joan was the driving force behind him. Whenever he got cold feet, she was there to urge him on.

By June 11, the French were camped outside Jargeau, a fortified town on the Loire west of Orléans. Reinforced by John of Dunois, the French had a total of eight thousand men.[10] Though enthusiastic, Joan and her army had little hard knowledge of the English garrison in Jargeau. More cautious leaders found reason to believe the enemy was stronger than the French, plus having the benefit of strong fortifications. Joan dismissed their fears. God, she told them, was conducting this campaign.[11] They could not lose.

After a seesaw fight in the outskirts of Jargeau, the French drove the English behind their walls. Cannon were brought up, and a bombardment began. La Hire, acting on his own, tried to talk the English commander, the Earl of Suffolk, into surrendering. The earl said he would if he was not relieved within fourteen days. Sir John Fastolf could reach Jargeau in that time. The earl was gambling on Sir John coming to their aid.

Joan vetoed La Hire's negotiations. The English could leave Jargeau if they surrendered at once, leaving behind their arms and equipment. Not surprisingly, the Earl of Suffolk refused.

The French assaulted the town. During the fight, the Maid had an inspiration and warned d'Alençon to shift his place. D'Alençon moved, and a soldier who stood in his place was promptly killed by a cannonball.

Joan's method of attack was basic and direct: The French stormed the walls with scaling ladders. She went up one of the first ladders herself, somehow carrying her famous banner as she climbed. An English soldier hurled a stone at her. It struck her on the helmet, sending her crashing to the ground.

Dazed, Joan got to her feet shouting, "Friends! Friends! Up, up! The Lord has condemned the English! This hour they are ours—be of good heart!"[12]

The French carried the battlement. They swarmed over the wall, overwhelming the earl's men. Suffolk was there in person, and he fled with the rest of his men to a bridge across the Loire. The earl was captured. Many of his men fell into the river in their haste to escape and drowned because of their heavy armor, as their comrades had at Orléans. The Duke d'Alençon estimated English losses at eleven hundred killed, with many prisoners taken.[13] Reports after the battle stated that many English prisoners were executed. It is not known to what extent this is true, or if Joan had any knowledge of it. It would have been out of character for her to order helpless men killed, though not for some of her captains, like the fierce La Hire.[14]

PUSHING THE ENGLISH BACK

Joan and the Duke d'Alençon journeyed to Orléans after the fall of Jargeau. There a gift awaited her, a red cloak and green tunic, gifts from the Duke of Orléans. The duke was a prisoner in England, but even there he heard of the Maid's exploits and had the clothing sent to Joan. It was more than mere finery. Red and green were the colors of the House of Orléans. Joan's acceptance of the tunic and cloak placed her firmly in the Armagnac camp.[15]

Joan rested no more than a day or two before pressuring d'Alençon to take the army downriver to free the next occupied town. Her injuries at Orléans had not dimmed her ardor. Rugged soldiers marveled at the peasant girl's resilience. Her noble commanders were annoyed by her constant demands to get after the English.

Together with her "good duke" d'Alençon and a handful of soldiers, Joan visited the English-held city of Meung on June 15, spying on the garrison there. English resistance must have impressed Joan, for she contented herself with seizing the bridge outside the city and leaving the town itself alone. Downstream, a more important target beckoned: Beaugency, another river town west of Blois. The English held a twelfth-century stone keep in the heart of Beaugency. Joan's army at once attacked the stronghold, blasting at the thick stone walls with their cannon.[16] That same day, June 16, Sir John Fastolf's army finally reached Janville, eighteen miles from Orléans and thirty miles from Beaugency.[17]

The French were in a very dangerous position, between the garrison of Beaugency and Sir John. Fortunately, reinforcements arrived, led by the despised Constable of France, Arthur de Richemont, who at one time had rebelled against the dauphin's authority. D'Alençon, John of Dunois, and other French lords considered de Richemont a traitor, but Joan welcomed him on condition he fight loyally for the dauphin. De Richemont agreed, adding his sizable command to Joan's force.[18]

Faced with a large army led by the infamous Maid of Orléans, the English in Beaugency asked for surrender terms. D'Alençon quickly accepted. The English were allowed to evacuate the keep with all their weapons and horses. As they rode away, La Hire's company brought word that Sir John Fastolf was close at hand.[19]

By now, Sir John was outnumbered and his command divided. Dispirited by the loss of Orléans, Jargeau, and Beaugency, half of Sir John's captains advised him to withdraw to Normandy and await reinforcement. The rest wanted to stand and fight. Sir John did not believe the French would allow him to simply march away, so on June 17, he offered battle a few miles from Meung. He followed the age-old tactics of Edward III, taking a defensive stance behind obstacles. Joan's army was not tempted to attack. The enemies glared at each other all day, but no battle ensued. Frustrated, Sir John took his men back to Meung.[20] The English commander intended to secure the bridge there, but word came Joan was coming after them. Afraid of being bottled up in the town, the English decided to retreat to Paris. Sir John divided his army into three parts (a standard practice in medieval armies), commanding the center, or main body, himself.

John of Dunois asked Joan if they should let the English go in peace, as they had the garrison of Beaugency. "Have good spurs," replied the Maid, meaning the French should give chase.[21]

Hard-driving La Hire took the advance guard and set off after Sir John. He caught up with the English near the town of Patay. Seeing he could not evade the French, Sir John chose a favorable site for the inevitable battle. Along a slope, he arranged his wagons and artillery to hamper any cavalry charge. Behind some thick hedges, he placed five hundred longbowmen. With this force in place, he sent the rest of his army on. Sir John only meant to fight a delaying action.[22]

It was a good plan. The hedges concealed the longbowmen, and if the French tried to attack the row of wagons, they would surely fall under a hail of arrows. At a critical moment, when La Hire's scouts were near, a deer emerged from the woods near the English line. The bowmen cheered and took a few shots at the beast, giving away Sir John's carefully arranged trap. French horsemen galloped through gaps in the hedges, catching the archers off guard and routing them. With that, the entire English line collapsed.[23] French knights chased the English out of their prepared positions and slaughtered them. Sir John Fastolf managed to elude capture, but the defeat marked the end of his military career. Most of the rank-and-file English soldiers were killed.[24] Only the highborn captives

Joan almost always wore a full suit of armor, just like the male soldiers around her.

were spared for ransom. The battle of Patay ended before Joan even arrived on the scene.

The terrible discrepancy of casualties seen at Crécy, Poitiers, and Agincourt was reversed at Patay. Estimates of English dead ranged from two to four thousand, with two hundred nobles taken prisoner. French losses (of knights, since commoners were not counted) amounted to just three.[25]

Orléans had been a surprising victory, but Patay stunned everyone. It was the first time in a very long time the French had defeated the English in open battle. The effects of Patay were far-reaching. French towns that had professed loyalty to the English quickly changed sides, proclaiming their allegiance to the dauphin. Some English outposts south of Paris were simply abandoned as indefensible. At a stroke, the Loire became French again. All this happened within two months of Joan's first arrival at Orléans.

Though Joan was not present at the battle, her army won the victory. The spirit she gave it, coupled with her will to succeed in her mission, inspired the French to overwhelm their longtime foes. The Duke d'Alençon, astonished at his own success, expressed amazement at his own triumph to his captured counterpart, Sir John Talbot.

Such are the fortunes of war, Sir John replied.[26] But war had never seen the like of Joan of Arc.

FROM DAUPHIN TO DIVINE KING

WITH THE LOIRE WON BACK FOR FRANCE, JOAN listened to her voices and announced it was time for the dauphin to journey to Reims to be crowned king. Of all the choices open to the royalists, crowning Charles was not high on the list. The warlords wanted to follow up Patay with an invasion of Normandy, and drive the enemy right into the English Channel. Given the shaken state of English leadership after Patay, such a bold move might have succeeded.

Paris, the greatest city in France and the center of French opposition to the dauphin, feared it was Joan's next target. On June 21, three days after the battle of Patay, panic struck the city when rumors that the royalist army, led by the Maid of Orléans, was at the city gates. Though the rumor proved false, it so rattled the city fathers that they ordered Paris' defenses strengthened.

It may surprise modern readers to hear that Paris, the quintessential French city, was so violently opposed to the legitimate heir to the French throne. The city fathers of Paris, along with the faculty of the university, were strongly against the dauphin and the Armagnac faction. They did not love the English so much as they hated the House of Valois, its staggering taxes, and the incompetent way so many Valois kings had ruled.

Joan was not concerned with Paris or Normandy yet. Her sacred mission was to see Charles crowned. The victories at Orléans and the Loire valley were glorious, but they were only a means to that end. The time was right to journey to Reims.

Why Reims? An ancient legend—which Joan believed to be true history—told how Saint Rémi baptized Clovis, King of the Franks, in Reims in A.D. 496. During the baptism ceremony, Saint Rémi noticed his supply of holy oil was almost exhausted. A dove descended from the sky bearing a vial of consecrated oil, with which Saint Rémi finished the rite. Ever after, the vial brought by the dove miraculously refilled itself when needed.[1] Saint Rémi was also the man Joan's home village, Domrémy, was named after. Historically speaking, kings of France from A.D. 1026 onward were crowned at Reims, establishing a tradition no French monarch could flout.

The dauphin agreed with Joan the moment had arrived to go to Reims. Though the route would take them through hostile territory, Charles believed Joan's success on the battlefield would compel his French enemies to come to terms with him. He saw the journey as a chance to win back French land without bloodshed.[2]

The day after Patay, June 19, Joan returned to Orléans. The dauphin had come to Sully, east of Orléans. Charles lingered at the castle of his favorite adviser, Georges de la Tremoille. Tremoille, a crafty, conniving character, had replaced Arthur de Richemont as the dauphin's chief minister. Joan and the prince met at St. Benoît-sur-Loire, west of Sully. Charles praised her lavishly, but when he expressed sympathy for the hardship she had suffered and suggested she take a rest, Joan wept. She thought she was being dismissed and vowed she would not rest until he was crowned king.[3]

The restless dauphin moved on to Gien, a town farther upriver that was a good starting point for a trip to Reims. Joan and the Duke d'Alençon arrived at Gien on June 24. She told the duke, "Have the trumpets sounded and mount your horse. It is time to go to gentle king Charles and set him on his way to his anointing at Reims."[4]

Before leaving, the dauphin dispatched letters to the towns along the route, reminding them of his recent victories and inviting the local gentry to his coronation. Joan sent letters too, enumerating the English lords she had defeated, killed, or captured. It was not unusual for a conqueror to boast, but Joan ascribed all her successes to God, not herself.

Joan also dictated a letter to the Duke of Burgundy, English ally and enemy of the dauphin. The territory between Gien and Reims was under Burgundian control. Joan had no desire to fight her way through to Reims, but she was prepared to do so. She did not threaten the duke but offered peace. Come to the coronation, she urged him.

Join the righteous side of the conflict and unite behind the rightful king of France.[5]

While Joan practiced her blunt but honest diplomacy, the dauphin became reluctant. His advisers frightened him with reminders of how many towns along the way to Reims were held by the English or Burgundians. Money was short. Time was short too, as Charles and Joan both had announced their intention to go to Reims without having planned the expedition in advance.

News of the dauphin's plight spread among his loyal subjects and a great outpouring of patriotism saved Joan. Knights, soldiers, and common people flocked to the dauphin's standard, ready to follow Joan to the coronation. Charles scraped together some money to pay his army. Nominal sums were given to each qualified soldier who volunteered. Knights and nobles had to support themselves, and commoners were on their own. The dauphin's infamous reluctance to spend money did not discourage anyone this time. So great was Joan's stature after her sweep through the Loire valley that an army of twelve thousand came to Gien to accompany her to Reims.[6]

This host moved out on June 29, 1429. Their first obstacle was the town of Auxerre, held by Burgundians. When Joan arrived, the gates were firmly shut against her. Some of her captains wanted to storm the town, but the dauphin's favorite adviser, Tremoille, concluded a deal that prevented violence. Auxerre's gates would remain closed, though the inhabitants agreed to sell food and supplies to Joan's army. If the larger cities of Troyes, Châlons, and Reims submitted to the dauphin, Auxerre would too, retroactively. This compromise did not please Joan, who wanted total submission to her prince. Later it was charged that Tremoille received two thousand crowns from the city fathers of Auxerre to spare their town.[7]

A Series of Bloodless Victories

On went the army to Troyes, a sizable town on the upper Seine River. A small English-Burgundian garrison emerged from the city to fight, but when they saw the size of Joan's army they quickly retreated inside, barring the gates. The town council did not want to fight the Maid and her great army, so they sent a delegation to negotiate terms. Leading the delegation was Brother Richard, a Franciscan monk who enjoyed a reputation as a popular preacher. Upon meeting the famous Maid of Orléans, Brother Richard made the sign of the cross and flung holy water at her, as though he was exorcising an evil spirit. Joan took this in good humor, replying, "Approach boldly! I shall not fly away."[8]

The monk knelt before her. Joan fell to her knees too, and they had a lengthy private conversation. When it was over, Brother Richard arose a convert. He told Joan and her followers he would return to Troyes and proclaim it was God's wish that they submit to the dauphin. Joan sent along a letter telling the nervous inhabitants of Troyes they had nothing to fear from her or her army if they accepted Charles in peace.

Despite Brother Richard and the Maid's letter, the town council was afraid of Joan, calling her "a madwoman full of the devil."[9] They sent warnings to Châlons and Reims, saying that the enemies of King Henry (Henry VI, king of England) and the Duke of Burgundy were on their way.

Not sure what to do, the dauphin held a council of his own. Members of his privy council attended, as did the noble commanders of the army—but not Joan. She was not invited. Without her single-minded clarity, Charles's meeting came to nothing. One of the dauphin's advisers recommended an immediate retreat to friendly territory. Others demanded Joan be consulted, and she was sent for. Striding boldly in, she declared they could capture Troyes in three days, "by love or by force." The Burgundians, unlike the English, had little direct experience with the Maid of Orléans. They were about to get it.[10]

Joan set her soldiers to preparing fascines, which were large bundles of sticks and brush used to fill in an enemy ditch, or trench. She directed them to throw the fascines into the moat surrounding Troyes. When the people in the city saw this, they knew a real attack was coming, one led by the victor of Orléans, Jargeau, and Patay. They surrendered at once. Charles entered Troyes in triumph, and Joan walked by his side, carrying her great banner.[11] The dauphin pardoned everyone in Troyes. Relieved, the city quickly handed over the supplies Joan's army required to continue its march.

On they went, winning one bloodless victory after another. Towns large and small submitted to the dauphin, but they were really surrendering to Joan of Arc, the Maid of Orléans. She adopted the simple tactic of sending her standard ahead of the army with a herald who proclaimed, "Surrender yourselves to the King of Heaven and to gentle King Charles."[12]

Châlons opened their gates without even a threat. While there, Joan met some people from Domrémy who had come to see the national figure she had become. She chatted with her one-time neighbors, allegedly telling a farmer named Epinal "she feared nothing but treason."[13]

This gloomy prediction, made on the eve of her greatest triumph, calls for some explanation. As long as Joan was fighting the English or the poor nerve of French military leaders, she was supremely confident. Since rejoining the dauphin, however, she had gotten a daily dose of political maneuvering, backroom dealing, and two-faced diplomacy. Charles's advisers, of whom Tremoille was the most influential, persisted in trying to find a nonviolent end to the long war with England and the struggle with Burgundy. Tremoille and company showed themselves willing to trade away almost anything for peace—even the dauphin's crown, if necessary. When Joan was added to the equation, several ugly truths emerged.

First, for all her honesty, devotion, and obvious military success, Joan was still a peasant girl. To Tremoille and other courtiers (as well as some of the dauphin's army officers) she did not belong at the dauphin's side or on the battlefield. Her presence in either place amounted to an upset of the natural order they believed in. No amount of victories could change that.

Nor were they comfortable with her claims of divine inspiration. Men of faith or not, French nobles knew well the dangers of making a commoner like Joan a hero. It was all very well for Saint Michael, Saint Catherine, and Saint Margaret to push Joan into making war on the English and seeing the dauphin crowned king. Once these matters were settled, then what? Would the voices tell Joan to seek redress for the many grievances of the common people of France? Peasants had revolted before during the Hundred Years War. Suppressing revolts was a bloody and costly business. How bloody and costly would it be if a peasant army arose, led by the Maid of Orléans? When it came to their opinions on politics and social order, the dauphin and his courtiers had more in common with English aristocrats like the Duke of Bedford or the captured Sir John Talbot than they did with a farmer's daughter from Domrémy.

Such were the questions circulating among the men of the dauphin's inner circle.[14] They shared their fears with Charles. Though the dauphin has been called cowardly, he was more calculating than fearful. He understood the situation as well as anyone. In the space of few months, the strange girl from Lorraine had shaken France to its foundations, reversed the tide of war, and brought Charles to the brink of kingship. As long as she adhered to her mission to see him made king and to evict the English from France, the dauphin would allow Joan her head. In a united and peaceful country, however, Joan might prove to be a problem.

A Coronation

On Saturday, July 16, 1429, the great procession arrived at Reims. It was hardly an army anymore, but a pilgrimage to see Charles's coronation. The crowd was also excited to see Joan of Arc standing in the ancient cathedral, her famous banner in hand.

Like the other cities along the way, Reims submitted meekly to the army at its gates. Joan and the dauphin entered as crowds of people cheered the spectacle of the long-denied prince and his savior proceeding to the great cathedral. The small English force that abandoned Reims before Joan arrived tried to sabotage the coronation by stealing the vestments and instruments from the cathedral.[15] Their effort failed in one critical way: They left behind the vial of holy oil of St. Rémi. When Joan's army took control of Reims, four senior commanders (the Marshal de Boussac, Admiral de Culan, Lord de Graville, and Gilles de Rais) were sent to secure the vial for the ceremony from the abbey of St. Rémi.[16] With a formidable array of clergymen in tow, the four paladins returned to the cathedral, where they rode their horses into the church, passing through the nave and dismounting by the choir.[17]

The cathedral was jammed with participants and spectators. Certain high nobles and prelates of the church were absent because their allegiance was to Burgundy. The Duke of Burgundy, though invited by Joan to attend the ceremony, did not appear. Lords loyal to the dauphin, including Joan's "good duke," d'Alençon, replaced the missing nobles.[18]

It was at this cathedral, Notre Dame de Reims, that Charles was crowned king in the presence of Joan.

The ancient ceremony proceeded. The Archbishop of Reims anointed Charles with the sacred oil. The Duke d'Alençon, acting as the senior peer, knighted the dauphin, then the archbishop placed the crown of France on Charles's head. Once Charles was crowned, the archbishop removed his miter (a tall cap) in recognition that the king now outranked him. He kissed Charles on both cheeks, and the loyal nobles in Charles's company did the same, bearing their heads and bowing to the new king.

Charles VII, as he was now, bestowed some titles in return. Guy de Laval and Georges de la Tremoille both were named counts. Gilles de Rais was made a marshal of France. D'Alençon knighted several young men who had distinguished themselves in battle.

The coronation was lengthy, starting at nine o' clock in the morning and lasting until two o'clock without pause. Through it all, Joan stood by her king, clad in bright armor and carrying her renowned flag.

When the ceremony concluded, the assembly shouted "Noel!" Trumpets blared a fanfare. Joan fell to her knees before Charles VII and embraced his legs, a gesture of extreme submission. Weeping, she declared "Gentle king, now is done God's pleasure, Who willed that I raise the siege of Orléans and that I bring you to this city of Reims to receive your holy sacring, showing that you are true King and him to whom the kingdom of Heaven should belong."[19]

This was the pinnacle of Joan's life. Even if she did not know what the future held, she could not fail to realize this was her finest hour.

TRUST NOT IN PRINCES

THE CROWNING OF CHARLES VII WAS NOT favorably received in Paris. Rouen was the seat of English power in France, but Paris was still the greatest city in the country and the center of French economic and intellectual life. The English, the Burgundians, and the French opposed to the Valois dynasty maintained an uneasy alliance, based solely on the fact they had a common enemy, Charles and the Armagnacs.

Now that the dauphin had been crowned king with all the pomp and ritual of the ancient throne of France, the three-way alliance began to show signs of strain. To many in the Burgundian faction, it seemed as if the Armagnacs had won. To the masters of Paris, there was the distinct possibility they might have to come to terms with Charles if his military and political successes continued. For the English, as foreign conquerors in a land not their own, treachery loomed everywhere. The dauphin's tense but remarkably nonviolent march to Reims demonstrated how easily the gains of thirty years of war could be undone.

Another casualty of the ceremony at Reims was Joan of Arc. With the crown firmly on Charles's head, a great part of her mission was over. Already behind her back the king's advisers were maneuvering to get rid of her.[1]

SHADY DIPLOMACY

Following the coronation, King Charles held a banquet for his loyal lords. The Duke d'Alençon was there, the Count de Clermont, and many other high nobles. Joan was not on the guest list. Aside from the dislike and distrust the king's ministers had for the upstart peasant girl, after the coronation Joan made herself unpopular by harassing the king to make an attack on Paris. The city had formidable defenses, and following the ceremony at Reims, it was heavily reinforced by the English, led in person by the regent, the Duke of Bedford.[2]

Joan tried her hand at diplomacy. She wrote a letter to the Duke of Burgundy, asking him to renounce his alliance with the English and make peace with Charles VII. If the duke must make war, she wrote, "go and wage it on the Saracens" (the Muslim rulers of the Holy Land).[3]

Philip the Good, Duke of Burgundy, responded with an offer of a truce of fifteen days. His soldiers would stand down, and at the end of the truce period, Paris would be delivered into Charles's hands.[4] Once that was done, more detailed negotiations could begin to heal the wounds between Armagnac France and Burgundy.

This was a masterful trick. Paris was not the duke's to give, since the English occupied it. The truce was accepted, but Joan was not fooled by Philip's offer. She sent a letter around to her followers, advising them not to expect to see her enter Paris anytime soon. At the end of the fifteen days, nothing had changed. Talks between the royalists and Burgundians came to nothing. Paris remained in English hands. Joan's letter to Philip and his proposal of truce accomplished nothing for her cause but allowed the Duke of Bedford extra time to strengthen the city's defenses.

Charles's army maneuvered along the Seine River, backing off when the English seized key bridges across the river. When the French seemed reluctant to engage, the Duke of Bedford sent a baiting letter to the newly crowned king of France.

The letter was long and insulting. Bedford challenged the French to face the English in open battle. He called Charles a murderer for his part in the plot to murder John the Fearless, Duke of Burgundy and father of Philip the Good. Bedford blamed Charles for all the ills that had befallen France. He reserved special scorn for the Maid of Orléans. He called her a "disorderly woman dressing as a man," implying an immoral purpose behind Joan's practical assumption of male attire while on campaign.[5] Bedford portrayed Joan as Charles's evil genius, the instigator of war and the suffering that followed.

Charles VII was used to being called names, so he ignored the Duke of Bedford's letter. Joan did not. Using her influence, she persuaded the king to let her take the royal army to Paris. She and the army made slow progress toward the city, and by August 14, 1429, the French were camped outside the town of Senlis, near Montépilloy. Bedford decided to strike them there. He had about nine thousand men to oppose Joan's six to seven thousand.[6] The two armies skirmished on the evening of the fourteenth, then prepared for battle the next day.

ATTACK ON PARIS

The French were confident. They had beaten the English several times in a row, and they had the Maid of Orléans with them. Bedford resorted to the same tactics Sir John Falstolf used to win the Battle of the Herrings. He surrounded his camp with trenches, stakes, and freight wagons. As the English had been doing since the days of Edward III, Bedford intended to fight a defensive battle to win an offensive action.

The resulting encounter was something of a farce. Though fought in deadly earnest, neither side would make the crucial mistake the other required. The English stayed inside their defenses. The French would not charge the deadly array of stakes and ditches, backed by waiting longbowmen. Joan tried to tease the enemy out by parading in plain sight before the French lines, but Bedford was not tempted. The battle of Montépilloy ended without any decision. The French returned to their camp, and the English marched away to Paris.[7]

It was not a stirring victory like Orléans or Patay, but Joan's progress toward Paris continued to harvest towns defecting from the English and Burgundians. Bedford had more problems as rebellion brewed in Normandy.

Charles VII left the army after Montépilloy, journeying to Compiègne where he was treated as a pampered guest. He lingered there until August 28, doing nothing to pursue Bedford or take Paris. Impatient with the delay, Joan continued to ask the king for permission to attack Paris. Charles's advisers, led by Tremoille, were against any move against the city. Unusually, Charles sided with Joan and gave her permission to go. She left Compiègne on August 23 with her usual commanders: d'Alençon, the Duke of Bourbon, Marshal de Rais, Marshal de Boussac, La Hire, and an unknown number of soldiers.[8]

Three days later, Joan and the royal army reached the outskirts of Paris. They encountered no resistance along the way. Joan halted at St. Denis, within sight of the city walls. There she and the king's commanders made their plans to storm the city.

While Joan prepared for her attack, Charles VII was quietly undercutting the work for which she was risking her life. A group of French prelates, led by Archbishop Regnault of Chartres, embarked on a mission of their own to reconcile Charles with Duke Philip of Burgundy. At Compiègne they found the king in a willing mood. Charles always favored diplomacy over warfare, and he was prepared to make concessions to Burgundy in order to pry apart the alliance between Philip the Good and England.

The rift between Armagnac and Burgundy had become open warfare as a result of the assassination of Philip's father in 1419.[9] Though Charles was not the instigator of the plot (Count Bernard of Armagnac was), he apparently knew about it and did nothing to stop it.[10] Once he became king and immune to ordinary prosecution, Charles took responsibility for the elder duke's death and offered territory to Burgundy in recompense, including the towns of Compiègne, Senlis, Creil, and Pont-Ste.-Maxence.[11] Joan would have been furious to know these towns, so recently reclaimed for the crown, were being given away to buy peace. Perhaps that's why Charles allowed her to go to Paris, in spite of his advisers' objections. At Paris, Joan was unable to interfere with the king's delicate negotiations.

Philip the Good accepted these terms and offered in return a four-month truce. He promised to stay neutral in any fight with the English. The agreement was signed August 28.

It was not worth the parchment it was written on. While dealing with Charles through Archbishop Regnault, Philip also concluded a deal with the English to supply them with more troops once the truce was over. The Duke of Bedford promised to make Philip Lieutenant of France and turn over the counties of Brie and Champagne to Burgundy.[12]

While Charles gave away hard-won land and Philip the Good prepared to stab his royal cousin in the back, Joan was facing the most formidable fortifications in western Europe. Paris had always been well protected, but during the reign of Charles V (1364–1380) the city walls had been massively reinforced. The walls Joan faced were twenty-six feet high. Every three hundred sixty feet or so great towers reared up. There were six gates, all fortified with thick walls and supplied with drawbridges, portcullises, arrow slits, and gun ports. The city was surrounded by a moat ten feet deep and up to a hundred feet wide at key places, fed by the Seine River.[13]

This was the city Joan chose to attack with any army of no more than seven thousand soldiers. Her plan resembled the English attempt to take Orléans by seizing a key gate and forcing an entry there. She chose the Porte St. Honoré, convenient to her camp at La Chapelle. Joan's method of identifying a weak point in the defense was naïve. She sent out bands of skirmishers to ride close to the walls, thereby measuring the response of the defenders at different points. It did not occur to her the defenders might ignore her diversions. During these probings, royal artillery bombarded the walls. Joan continued testing Paris's defenses for several days while waiting the arrival of Charles VII.[14]

Charles delayed coming until September, arriving at St. Denis on the seventh. He was practically dragged there by the Duke d'Alençon. The next day, Joan led her men against the Porte St. Honoré. With Gilles de Rais and Raoul de Gaucort at her side, she tried to ford the moat (the water level was low, but it was mired with mud) with her assault. Overhead cannon roared, and arrows flew thick and fast from both sides. The attack began at noon and lasted until sunset without resolution. Then, as the light was failing, Joan was hit in the thigh by a crossbow bolt. Arrows killed her standard bearer, standing beside her. Wounded, she raised her voice even louder, urging her enemies to yield: "You must surrender to us quickly, for

Jesus's sake, for if you do not surrender yourselves before it becomes night, we will invade you by force, willing or not, and you will be put to death without mercy!"[15] Despite her bravado, the royalists fell back. Defenders on the wall taunted them. Joan attracted a great deal of scorn and obscenity. Stung, she refused to retreat, though badly hurt. In the end, Lord de Gaucourt had her carried to safety against her will.

The royal army prepared to renew the assault the next day, in spite of Joan's wound. Before the attack got under way, Joan was summoned to St. Denis by the king. Charles VII had grave doubts that any assault could succeed against the powerful defenses, and he called off the attack over the protests of Joan, the Duke d'Alençon, and the other captains. Charles was right about Paris being too strong to take by storm, but he was probably thinking of his secret deal with Burgundy too. Four months of truce would allow him to build up the army again, perhaps to invade Normandy as his advisers wished. Throwing his most loyal soldiers against stone walls was a waste, so Charles called it off. On September 12, 1429, the royal army marched away from Paris. The Maid of Orléans had failed for the first time.

When the army departed, Joan left her armor behind as a gift to the cathedral of St. Denis. It is not clear if she meant this as thanks to Our Lady of St. Denis for her survival or as a way of apology for the decision to retreat.

Joan courageously led the siege of Paris but was ultimately defeated. This illustration from the Renaissance incorrectly shows her wearing a dress.

THE KING DISTANCES HIMSELF

Joan's aura of invincibility was shattered by her first defeat. Repulsed at Paris, the royal army withdrew, not northward near the English, but south, back to the safer Loire valley. As the army retreated, small garrisons were left behind, commanded by officers loyal to Charles VII rather than Joan's followers. Many of these small towns were soon reoccupied by English or Burgundian troops, and the consequences for the people who had so joyfully welcomed Joan only months before were harsh.[16]

Even more startling was the king's decision on September 21 to dissolve the army. The Duke d'Alençon was sent home to his family. D'Alençon tried to persuade the king to send Joan to him later for a proposed invasion of Normandy, but Charles refused. The Duke d'Alençon never saw Joan of Arc again.[17]

Kept at the king's court at Gien, Joan yearned for action. The inactivity wore on her nerves. She told the Archbishop of Reims she might as well go home to Domrémy and tend her father's sheep again.[18] She probably did not mean it. A large part of her mission—the expulsion of the English from France—was still not done. She sat idle at Charles VII's court, the least suitable place for her in the world.

This was the time of the four-month truce with Burgundy. Joan constantly agitated to be sent somewhere to fight. The king and his advisers would not let her join d'Alençon in an attack on Normandy. She urged another attack on Paris, which was also vetoed. Like a caged lion, Joan followed the royal court to Bourges, with nothing to do but harass the king for an opportunity to fight his enemies.

Charles VII was in no mood to fight anyone. He was broke. He was the true king of France, but he had no money and little chance of raising any in his current situation. For this reason alone he was reluctant to set Joan loose. There was no money for any army. Moreover, he believed his diplomats and his councillor Tremoille would bring him bloodless successes that he would not owe to Joan.

A Defeat and a Premonition

In October, Charles found work for Joan. Her leg wound was on the mend, so he sent her to St. Pierre-le-Moutier to suppress a mercenary band under the command of Perrinet Gressart. Gressart served the Duke of Burgundy, and he held a considerable part of the upper Loire region under his personal control. Gressart was little more than a gangster. He once captured Georges de la Tremoille and held him for a heavy ransom. Tremoille paid, but he never forgot the insult. It is easy to imagine he would favor sending the Maid after his old captor. Whoever won, the gangster or the peasant girl, Tremoille would be happy with the result.[19]

With a small company of soldiers, Joan left Bourges in late October 1429. She captured one of Gressart's lesser towns, but the effort drained her army's meager resources to the extent she could not mount a proper siege of Gressart's fortress at La Charité-sur-Loire. It was winter, and after a month's siege, Joan had to give up. Even the Maid of Orléans could not win without food, supplies, and gunpowder.

Defeated, she returned to Jargeau around New Year's Day 1430. There she learned her family had been ennobled by the king and given the name Du Lys. It must have seemed like a poor reward considering her recent failures.[20]

Joan's activities in the early weeks of 1430 are obscure. She avoided the king's court with its worldly vanities and ever-present intrigue. Letters survive that she had dictated to the people of Reims, who felt themselves under threat from Burgundy. She reassured them Charles VII would not abandon them, and they should resist any attempt by collaborators within the city to welcome back the Burgundians.[21]

The king lingered in the Loire valley, moving from one castle to another during the winter of 1430. Though Charles appeared uninterested in liberating more of this kingdom, the people of France had not lost the spark given them by the Maid of Orléans. There were uprisings against the English and Burgundians in St. Denis, Melun, and a sizable plot within Paris. The last conspiracy was crushed when 150 patriots were arrested. Six were executed for trying to deliver Paris to the rightful king of France.[22]

Things were ugly in Compiègne. Charles VII had promised to return Compiègne to Burgundian rule as part of his reconciliation with Duke Philip. This was easier said than done. The people of Compiègne didn't want to revert to Burgundian control. The commander of the French garrison, Guillaume de Flavy, prepared to resist Burgundian occupation. Charles's deputy in the region, Charles de Bourbon, told the Duke of Burgundy the people of Compiègne preferred war to submitting to his authority.[23] Philip the Good needed Compiègne badly. It was a strategic crossing of the Oise River, and for his upcoming campaign in concert with the English, he needed Compiègne in his hands. Philip's army moved on Compiègne. The pretense of neutrality was gone.

This was news Joan wanted to hear. She told confidants there could be no reconciliation with the enemies of France "except at lance point."[24] Without the king's permission, she set out toward Compiègne to get a firsthand look at the situation. By March 29, she was in the town of Lagny, where a purported miracle occurred. A baby had died without baptism, which according to church doctrine condemned the child's soul to purgatory. Joan held the baby, and it came back to life just long enough to be baptized.

On Easter 1430, her voices gave her a disturbing revelation. Her enemies would soon capture her.[25] Since she believed in her voices without question, she accepted the prophecy. Somberly, Joan carried on. On April 24 she arrived at Senlis.

English and Burgundian forces were converging on the Oise River. Philip the Good took the city of Choisy on May 16 and pushed a bridge across the river so he might link up with the English. To save Compiègne and prevent this conjunction of France's enemies, Joan of Arc led her small company to the Oise. There destiny awaited her on the bridge outside Compiègne on May 24, 1430.

SOLD TO THE HIGHEST BIDDER

WAR HAD BEEN THE MAKING OF JOAN, AND IT was her unmaking as well. Like a gambler who sticks in a game too long, her winning streak ran out. After she failed to capture Paris or subdue the mercenary Perrinet Gressart, her failure to lift the siege of Compiègne might have wrecked her reputation and her cause. Ironically, being captured by the Burgundians caused a fresh sensation throughout Europe. Everyone wondered, what would become of her now?

Upon hearing Joan had been taken by his troops, the Duke of Burgundy came to Margny, where she was being held, and paid the Maid of Orléans a visit. What passed between them was not recorded. A Burgundian at the meeting said the duke "said some words to her which I can't remember."[1] What Joan might have said to the duke can be imagined, but her words were not preserved either.

Joan was turned over to the Lionel of Wandomme's overlord, John of Luxembourg, who carried her off to his

90

camp at Claroix. A few days later, fearing a surprise attack by Joan's followers, Luxembourg had her removed to his castle at Beaulieu, near Noyon. Lionel of Wandomme was put in command of the castle, becoming Joan's jailer.[2]

Like lightning, news of the Maid's downfall reached Paris on May 25. The next day, the University of Paris and the Inquisitor of France sent a letter to Philip the Good demanding Joan be brought before the clerical faculty and the Inquisition. Everyone knew about her claims that she communicated with saints and angels. To the learned churchmen, the notion that Saint Michael, Saint Margaret, and Saint Catherine would converse with an unlettered farm girl smacked of heresy. Coupled with her unbelievable deeds on the battlefield, they thought it would be easy to bring charges of heresy and witchcraft against Joan.[3] The Parisian churchmen wanted to move quickly, lest Joan be rescued or ransomed.

Ransom was a common process in those days. Important captured nobles were seldom kept prisoner very long or killed. They were too valuable for such wasteful treatment. Joan was not of noble blood (though her family had recently been elevated by Charles VII), so it remained to be seen whether she would rot in a dungeon, be put to death, or be ransomed. Another question was, who would pay for the prize—Charles VII, to get his Maid back, or England, to make certain she never troubled English interests in France again?

By medieval law and tradition, the person who captured a valuable prisoner was entitled to the largest share of the ransom. The man who actually dragged Joan off her horse and forced her to surrender, an archer named Lyonnel, was in the service of the Lionel of Wandomme.[4] Lionel commanded a company of six men at arms and sixty-two yeomen under John of Luxembourg. Luxembourg owed allegiance to Philip the Good, Duke of Burgundy. The duke had an arrangement with King Henry VI of England to hand over any high-ranking French prisoners he might take, up to and including Charles VII. Therefore, it could be argued the English already had a claim to Joan.[5]

Complicating matters further were the ambitions of Pierre Cauchon, Bishop of Beauvais. The bishop had jurisdiction over Joan's home village of Domrémy in matters of Church law, not the Inquisition in Paris. Joan's speaking with voices and her pronouncements about God certainly had attracted the scrutiny of the Catholic Church. When Joan was taken at Compiègne, it meant the infallibility of her voices had become suspect.

As a Frenchman, a cleric, and a paid agent of the king of England, Cauchon was the perfect foil for the English to use to eliminate Joan. Being French, he could avoid the appearance of foreign animosity. Being a bishop instead of a soldier, he could pose as a man of God seeking justice, not a warlord seeking revenge. Finally, Cauchon's loyalty to the English cause was unquestioned. He could be counted on to deliver the verdict his English masters wanted.

ESCAPE ATTEMPTS

While pro-English church authorities clamored for Joan, she was taken from Beaulieu castle to an even more imposing fortress, Beaurevoir, near St. Quentin. Joan had tried to escape from Beaulieu and had almost succeeded. She pried up the floorboards of her cell and squeezed through the joists. She got as far as the ground floor, where she locked her guards in their tower. Before she could get away, however, the night watchman caught her.[6]

At Beaurevoir, John of Luxembourg put his resourceful captive in the care of three women he trusted completely—all named Joan, by coincidence—Joan of Luxembourg, his elderly aunt; Joan of Bethune, his wife; and Joan de Bar, Luxembourg's step-daughter. All three took a liking to the sturdy warrior girl. They treated her with vigilance and respect. They also tried to convince Joan to put aside her male attire and wear a dress, but she refused. God would not permit her to resume female dress until her mission was done, she said.[7]

Joan had more practical reasons to retain her soldier's outfit. She intended to escape, a feat more suited to tunic and hose than a huge medieval gown.

A few weeks into her captivity at Beaurevoir, she tried to get away again. Her second attempt was more desperate than the first: She leaped from a high tower. Joan jumped from the top of the tower whose height has been estimated at least sixty feet. She fell hard, knocking herself unconscious. It was a miracle she was not killed. When Joan awoke, she had no memory of what happened (perhaps a symptom of concussion) and the Burgundian guards told her she had jumped.[8] Without so much as a broken bone or sprained ankle to show for it, Joan felt she had been spared for some greater purpose.

Her leap may have been an escape, but some thought it may have been a suicide attempt. She denied the latter charge, but said she tried the stunt to keep out of the hands of the vengeful English and "to help the people of Compiègne."[9] During her recovery, Saint Catherine appeared, telling Joan to ask forgiveness of God for risking her own life.

Since Beaurevoir had not proved secure enough, Joan was moved again to Arras. She was held in a house belonging to the Duke of Burgundy. Joan of Luxembourg, who had come to admire the Maid during her four months at Beaurevoir, begged her nephew, John of Luxembourg, not to sell Joan to the English.[10]

JOAN'S PRICE

While Joan was languishing in captivity, Pierre Cauchon was busy trying to get her delivered into his hands. He traveled ceaselessly from Beaurevoir to Calais (to consult the English) to Flanders (where the Duke of Burgundy was), trying to convince his masters he was the man to settle accounts with the Maid of Orléans. Efficient bureaucrat that he was, he submitted a request to the English for 765 pounds to cover his travel expenses on their behalf. It was paid.[11]

To buy Joan, the English levied a special tax on the people of Normandy. They had to raise 120,000 pounds for the continuation of the war. Ten thousand pounds of this money was set aside in the budget to buy Joan of Arc "who is said to be a sorceress, a military person leading the dauphin's armies."[12] The people of France were being made to pay the blood money needed to deliver Joan into the hands of her enemies.

On November 21, 1430, Joan was transferred to the fortress of Le Crotoy, on an island in the English Channel. She was there about a month while the final deal for her handover to the English was struck. Ten thousand pounds was parceled out to those who had captured her. It was decided that Joan would be tried at Rouen, headquarters of the English army in France. Paris churchmen would have liked to have had her in their city, but Paris seethed with royalist rebellion. The presence of the Maid of Orleans there might spark a revolt, so the eighteen-year-old girl was packed off to Rouen, surrounded by most of the English army.

On December 20, 1430, Joan was taken across the Somme River estuary from Le Crotoy. Three days later, she was in Rouen, awaiting her trial.

TRIAL AND ERRORS

THE BIG QUESTION ASKED AT THE TIME OF Joan's capture, and asked repeatedly ever since, was why did Charles VII not do more to free her? Since he did virtually nothing to help Joan, people then and now have criticized the king for being ungrateful, false, and too tightfisted to ransom the woman who set the crown of France on his head.

It is easy to paint Charles as weak and dominated by his advisers, many of whom did not like or trust Joan. But this was also the man judged by his people to be "sweet-tempered, gracious, full of pity and mercy, a fine person of fine carriage and high understanding."[1] A sensitive man, Charles was ill equipped by his personality to lead a nation engaged in a brutal three-way war. He feared violence, and he usually sought diplomatic means to avoid it. His treasury was empty, so he could hardly bid for Joan's freedom, though he had assets he might have pawned. The English paid for Joan by taxing the people of Normandy.

Charles might have raised ransom money with a "save the Maid" tax. There were many in France who would have subscribed willingly to such a plan. Another question is why didn't any of Joan's very rich comrades in arms, like Gilles de Rais, offer to ransom her.

Ultimately the question of ransom did not matter. Her enemies had Joan, and they were not going to let her go for any sum of money. Charles VII knew this, but his failure to even try to buy Joan back shows he did not care enough about her. His reputation down through history had suffered accordingly.

A prisoner exchange was mentioned. Thanks to Joan's victories in the Loire valley, several high-ranking Englishmen were French prisoners: the Earl of Suffolk, taken at Jargeau, and Sir John Talbot, captured after the battle of Patay. Both men were experienced war leaders, but exchanges only happen if both sides are willing to make the swap. Joan's captors were not going to let her go for any lost warlord. She was only a teenage peasant girl from Lorraine, but her spirit had galvanized the French people at a time when the demise of France seemed imminent. She alone made possible the victories at Orléans and the Loire valley. She alone drove the reluctant dauphin to undertake the journey to Reims to be crowned. Joan was far too dangerous for the English to allow her to live.

This much is proven by a letter written on January 3, 1431, over the name of Henry VI, King of England (though written by one of his advisers). The letter said, "It is our intention to recover and take back . . . Joan if . . . she be not convicted or attainted of the case [of heresy]."[2]

Her fate was sealed the moment the archer dragged her from her horse at Compiègne. The only real question now was, how would Joan spend her days?

Her treatment by the Burgundians had been quite humane. In spite of her escape attempts, Joan was allowed to walk the battlements of her prison. At Beaurevoir, she was watched over by three noblewomen, who spent enough time with Joan so that they actually came to admire her. All this ended when she arrived in Rouen.

Her hands and feet were shackled with heavy chains. The leg irons were fastened to a heavy timber four feet long. She could not walk unaided and could barely stand in her bonds. The prison at Rouen had rooms set aside for female prisoners, but the vengeful English put Joan in a dank ordinary cell. She was guarded at all times by five soldiers drawn from the ranks of the English army, men who were rude, tough, and crude.

Joan had managed to tame the coarse behavior of the French soldiers she led. Her dignity, honesty, and strong faith convinced French soldiers to follow her example. She had no such influence over her captors. They cursed her, constantly made obscene remarks, and would not leave her alone even for her normal bodily functions.[3] The English guards played cruel games with her, telling her one day she was to be freed, on other days her execution had been set. A constant threat of rape hovered over Joan. She would declare at her trial one reason she kept wearing men's clothes in prison was to forestall molestation.

The English had an iron cage built to display Joan in at her trial, but it was not used.[4] However much they hated

Joan, and however much they wanted to humiliate her, someone on the English side must have realized showing her shackled in a cage would more likely generate sympathy for the prisoner.

One of Joan's first acts at Rouen was to ask for a physical examination. Joan knew her virginity was a vital part of her defense, as well as being central to people's belief in her mission. She was accused of being a witch, and since witches were said to have intercourse with demons, proof of virginity would undermine any such charges. Her claims to have had frequent contact with angels and saints likewise would be doubted if she had not led a pure life.

Anne of Burgundy, Duchess of Bedford, wife of the English regent and sister of Duke Philip the Good, conducted the examination.[5] The duchess and several matrons duly examined Joan in early January 1431. All attested to her virginity. The duchess thereafter ordered the guards that Joan was not be touched. Despite orders from so high a lady, the soldiers continued to torment their prisoner, to the point that Joan once had to cry out to her jailer, the Earl of Warwick, for help warding them off. Had the earl not come, Joan told her judges, she would have been raped.[6]

Outside the prison, Pierre Cauchon was still attempting to try Joan for heresy. Since heresy was a crime under Church law, Joan should have been held in a church prison, guarded by matrons, instead of being chained in a dungeon like a prisoner of war. Cauchon excused English barbarity by citing the fact that the door to Joan's cell had

PIERRE CAUCHON, BISHOP OF BEAUVAIS

Cauchon was the product of the University of Paris, a hotbed of anti-Armagnac thinkers. He had a brilliant career at school and moved up steadily through the ranks of the church hierarchy. He had attached himself to the Duke of Burgundy by 1412, going so far as to organize a revolt in Paris against the dauphin. Banished, Cauchon continued to work for the Burgundian faction. He accepted church posts from the self-proclaimed king of France, Henry V of England, and in 1420 he became Bishop and Count of Beauvais. Loyal to the English and Burgundian cause, Cauchon was kicked out of Beauvais by a popular uprising in 1429, inspired by Joan's successes in the Loire valley.[7]

three locks, one for each of the leading clergymen who were to be her prosecutor and judges. Thus while Joan was in a military prison, she was technically under the control of church authorities.[8]

Why was Joan tried for heresy? Partly this was arranged because the anti-Armagnac faction in Paris was centered among the faculty (clergymen all) at the University of Paris. They wanted to try Joan as the proxy of Charles VII, who was not likely to put himself in their hands. Also, the English wanted Joan dead. They could not simply execute her. She was a prisoner of war, and even in 1431 there were rules for the treatment of enemy combatants. Had the English killed Joan outright, many English prisoners in French hands would have suffered in retaliation.

Most of all, the English, the Burgundians, and their collaborating churchmen wanted to kill the *legend* of Joan. She had performed mighty deeds and saved Charles VII from obscurity and France from extinction, all the while citing God as the source of her success. People all over France looked to Joan of Arc as their national savior. If her enemies could destroy the image of Joan, they could undo the work she had done. Convicting her of heresy meant proving her voices were demons or delusions. It also would mean Joan's accomplishments were false, illicit, and rooted in evil. Lastly, a heresy conviction would allow them to execute her with all the weight of Church law. Execution for heresy was not only legal, it was officially an act of virtue.

And so Joan went to trial. She faced two judges, Pierre Cauchon, Bishop of Beauvais, and Jean Lemaistre, vicar of the Inquisitor of France. Though the priests, monks, and lawyers who filled the courtroom were often referred to as judges, officially there were only these two.[9] Cauchon, a canny politician, was Joan's most implacable enemy. Lemaistre was a different sort. Cautious, timid, he often did not approve of Cauchon's methods, but the Bishop of Beauvais easily dominated him. As the trial went on, Lemaistre grew more and more unhappy with the irregularities committed in the Church's name.[10] He found reasons to be absent, and when he did attend the trial, he seldom asked questions or made his presence felt.[11]

At any given time there were up to sixty "assessors" in court who were Norman and English clergymen, lawyers, clerks, and church court officials of various types. The University of Paris sent a team to the trial to make sure its interests were observed. They would prove to be Joan's severest critics.

The trial opened January 9. The court was assembled, and inquests were held in Domrémy and Vaucouleurs to collect testimony on Joan's early activities. The court met twice more to examine the material gathered from Lorraine, and two sessions followed involving the reluctance of Jean Lemaistre to participate in the trial.[12]

Joan was presented to the court at its first public session on Wednesday, February 21. The session began at 8 A.M. in the chapel of Rouen castle.[13] The court's first act was to review Joan's petition to be allowed to attend mass. Cauchon refused, citing her offense of wearing men's clothing. Until she renounced this unnatural practice, she would not be allowed to attend any church services.

Joan was led into the chapel. She was sworn in and told to speak the whole truth. She replied, "I do not know what you wish to examine me on. Perhaps you might ask such things that I would not tell."[14]

Cauchon rephrased the question. Would she answer truthfully about questions of the faith?

She said she would answer truthfully about religious matters, such as what her parents taught her as a child about the Catholic faith, but she would not discuss the revelations she had received from God. She had never discussed these with anyone, except Charles VII, her king. Even if it meant her death, Joan refused to reveal what her voices actually said to her. If her voices gave her leave to answer, she would, but not until then.

Exasperated, the bishop put it another way: Would she answer the court's questions truthfully on matters of doctrine? In answer, Joan knelt, put both hands on the Bible, and swore to answer the court's questions on doctrine truthfully, but she would not betray her voices.[15]

THE QUESTIONING BEGINS

The court's first questions were routine inquiries about her name, origins, and life growing up in Domrémy. When asked how old she was, Joan said that she thought she was nineteen. Asked about basic Catholic rituals like the Credo, Ave Maria, and Paternoster, Joan told the court she would not repeat them unless the court would hear her confession.[16]

These opening maneuvers set the tone for much of the trial. Joan answered firmly, at times defiantly. She knew the judges would try to trap her into admitting heretical beliefs, and she vigorously avoided their ploys.

At the session on February 22, Jean Beaupère, canon of Rouen cathedral and one-time chancellor of the University of Paris, questioned Joan about her voices.[17] She provided an account of her first visitation. In clear, uncomplicated language she related how the voices told her to raise the siege of Orléans. To do this, she must first go to Robert de Baudricourt (mentioned by the voices by name), the royalist commander stationed near Domrémy. De Baudricourt would give her men to accompany her to

Orléans. Joan tried to beg off, telling the voices she was only a poor woman who knew nothing of war. The voices insisted, and she obeyed.[18]

Who told her dress in men's clothing, asked Beaupère?

"I charge nobody."[19] By this Joan refused to implicate anyone, mortal or spiritual. She went on to explain that her travels through war-torn France made it necessary to wear men's clothes, both for ease of travel and to avoid molestation.

When asked about her famous meeting with the dauphin at Chinon, Joan became tight-lipped. Did her voices tell her how to recognize Charles?

"Pass on to the next question."

Did she see an invisible angel hovering over the dauphin?

"Spare me that," she replied sarcastically. "Continue."[20]

Here was no frightened girl, overawed by the high prelates around her. Joan had hobnobbed with kings and princes, and she had commanded dukes and counts in battle. She had seen hundreds of men die around her. Knowing she could not hope for mercy from paid agents of the English crown, she chose to be forthright, honest, and proud.

Beaupère pressed her for details of her private conversation with Charles. She would reveal nothing. She cut off the discussion by telling Beaupère to go to Charles VII and ask him what was said.

One interesting detail she did admit was hearing her voices every day. The trial transcript says "there is not a day when she does not hear this voice; and she has much need of it."[21] At the next session Beaupère interrogated her again and asked when she had last heard her voices. Yesterday and today, Joan replied. All she would reveal of the voices' messages was that they urged her speak boldly.

Boldly she spoke. For hours Joan stood before the court—forty to sixty educated, opinionated men—and gave brisk answers. She steadfastly refused to utter incriminating statements about her voices. She would not describe what she saw in her visions either, especially when the court tried to prize out absurd or erroneous descriptions of Saint Michael, Saint Margaret, or Saint Catherine. The judges wondered how she knew the visions she saw and heard were actual saints and not deceptions of the Devil? Joan could only reply she knew her voices told the truth. Everything they predicted came true. The saints were glorious and beautiful, and when they left "I fain [wish] would have had them take me with them."[22]

The judges asked silly questions, intended to make Joan sound insane or foolish. How did her holy visitors look? How did they smell? What did they wear? Some of her answers were priceless. When asked if Saint Michael appeared nude, Joan retorted, "What, do you think that God doesn't have the wherewithal to give him clothes?"[23]

Cauchon gradually abandoned the issue of Joan's voices. She kept refusing to answer any query she felt would incriminate her, so the court could make little headway on the subject. The subject of witchcraft never came up in any serious way after Joan's childhood was discussed. While her deeds were marvelous, there was no evidence to support the popular belief among the English that Joan was a witch. Her virginity alone counted deeply against any suspicion of witchcraft.

Though the court asked hundreds of questions—some simple, some confusing—Joan answered directly. Some of the men present were impressed and said so. She gave ample evidence of her intelligence, wit, and strong memory, all of which told against the idea she was deluded or insane. At one point, court member Boisguillaume insisted Joan had not been asked a certain question she said she had already addressed. Joan demanded the minutes be checked, and she was proved right. She told Boisguillaume if he made another such mistake she would pull his ears.[24]

By April 2, many of the original charges against Joan had been dropped. The list of seventy counts shrank to twelve, some of which were minor matters, such as believing in her apparitions without proof.[25] The entire case came to hinge on just two charges: that Joan willfully donned men's clothes in defiance of Church law, and that she defied the Church Militant.

The Church Militant is a Catholic term (still used) that refers to the earthly membership of the church. Every Catholic, whether a lay person, priest, or the pope, is a member of the Church Militant. The worldly church's counterpart in heaven is the Church Triumphant. God, his angels, the saints, and the souls of all those who die in the good graces of the church form the Church Triumphant.

Joan was accused of denying the role and the authority of the Catholic Church. By talking to angels and saints directly, she was putting herself in the role of a priest. When she took the word of her voices as the truth, she was denying the learned clergy their divinely ordained role as messengers between the people and God. The crucial point came when she was asked in the case of contradictory judgments, whom would she believe, the Church or her voices? Without hesitation, Joan said she would heed her voices in all things: "In case the Church wished her to do something contrary to the commandments she said came from God, she could not do it."[26]

As for wearing men's clothes, Joan could hardly deny it. She was wearing male attire before the court for all to see. Pressured on this point, Joan replied, "Everything I have done is at God's command; and if He had ordered me to assume a different habit, I should have done it, because it would have been His command."[27] Wearing men's clothes was both illegal and heretical. Besides the inference of homosexuality, wearing clothes of the opposite sex was prohibited based on Old Testament law. Deuteronomy 22:5 says "The woman shall not wear that which pertaineth unto a man, neither shall a man put on a woman's garment: for all that do so are abomination unto the Lord thy God."

In mid-April Joan fell sick, not surprising considering the conditions under which she was kept. She received prompt medical attention and recovered. Her jailer, the Earl of Warwick, remarked, "The King of England had paid too much for her to be deprived of the pleasure of seeing her burn."[28]

The twelve charges of heresy and Joan's answers on them were sent to sixteen doctors of theology and six leading lawyers, many from the hostile University of Paris. They were asked to evaluate the reduced charges and Joan's replies. Three days after receiving the court's report, the panel declared Joan guilty on all twelve counts.

Cauchon and Lemaistre presented the learned panel's findings and asked the prisoner if she would recant her stance (change her mind) on the heretical points. Joan refused. Several members of the court became concerned Joan was throwing her life away by refusing to accept the authority of the Church Militant. More concerned with saving her soul than convicting a heretic, three members of the court visited Joan in her cell and advised her to ask for a judgment by the pope. The advantage of this was obvious—the pope outranked Cauchon and could overrule the bishop's verdict. There were also men on the pope's council friendly to Charles VII and Joan's cause.[29] When Joan mentioned a papal appeal in court the next day, Cauchon blew up, demanding to know who had coached her to ask for it. The guards identified the culprits. Cauchon denounced them as meddlers and promised retribution. One fled Rouen. The other two applied for Lemaistre's protection, which he gave. Thereafter, no one from the court but Cauchon was allowed to see Joan.[30]

Cauchon turned the idea of papal judgment against her. Since she would not submit to the Church Militant as represented by him, would she submit to the pope and his cardinals?

Joan replied, "Take me there and I will ask him."[31]

The weight of Church law began to bear down on Joan. Found guilty of heresy, she was given a chance to recant and be spared. She stoutly refused to deny her voices or to give up her male clothing until her mission was accomplished. For refusing, Joan could now be legally tortured. The first step in the process was carried out. She was shown the instruments of torture on May 9.[32] Having come this far, it was Cauchon who backed down. He officially ruled out torture, claiming it would not serve justice to force a confession from Joan. Unofficially, the bishop knew the only ways to put a heretic to death were if the heretic refused to recant, or if after confessing, the heretic lapsed into heresy again. Cauchon therefore laid a trap for Joan, one she could not—or would not—avoid.

JOAN'S CONFESSION

On May 24, Joan was taken to the cemetery of St. Ouen in Rouen to hear a sermon by the rector of the University of Paris, Guillaume Erard. His text, and the court's message, was taken from John 15:6: "If a man abide not in me, he is cast forth as a branch, and is withered; and men gather them, and cast them into the fire, and they are burned." Nearby stood the executioner.[33]

At this point, Joan faltered for the first time. If she refused to recant her heresy now, she would burn then and there. She asked to submit to the judgment of the pope. She was told the pope was too far away and that his authority was delegated to the bishops now judging her.

The Cardinal of Winchester watched as Joan prayed to St. Michael. This work was painted by Paul Delaroche in 1824 and hangs in the Musee des Beaux-Arts in Rouen, France.

Clasping her hands in front of her, Joan prayed aloud to Saint Michael for guidance. Cauchon deferred to the senior churchman present, Cardinal Beaufort of Winchester, an Englishman, as to what to do. Beaufort told him to accept Joan as a penitent. She had officially recanted.

A written document was given to her to sign. She protested she could not read or write. A priest acting as an usher at the trial, Jean Massieu, explained the document to her. It was only six or seven lines long, Massieu later recalled. The confession supposedly signed by Joan that was inserted into the court record was over forty lines long.[34] The short version mentioned only that Joan swore to refrain from bearing arms and wearing male clothing. The longer version she apparently never saw also asks her to confess to "superstitious divination, cross-dressing, presumption, sedition, idolatry," while begging for the forgiveness of the Church.[35]

Joan signed with a scrawled mark, a circle or a cross. Now that she had confessed her error, she had to be forgiven. Many in the crowd thought this meant she would go free. English partisans in the crowd jeered and threw stones. Joan expected to be turned over to a church prison, but Cauchon ordered her back to her cell. Her English guards yelled at her as they escorted her back to Rouen castle.

The English leaders present were outraged. Cauchon had betrayed their trust, they said. The Maid of Orléans would not be burned at the stake. The Earl of Warwick complained this was not the outcome they had paid for.

One of the French clerics said, "My lord, do not trouble; we shall soon have her again."[36]

CONSIGNED TO FLAME

JOAN WENT BACK TO HER CELL. SHE WAS chained again to the crippling timber, and her five guards took up their places again, three inside the cell with her, two outside in the passage.[1] Outside, Rouen was in an uproar as the English protested Joan's "escape." She probably heard none of it. Deep inside Rouen castle, Joan received important visitors. Judge Lemaistre, with four assessors from the court, came to remind her she must not break her word to the Holy Mother Church. If she lapsed into heresy again, there would be no reprieve.

They also brought her a set of woman's clothes. Joan put them on, probably the first time she had worn female garments since leaving Vaucouleurs for Chinon in February 1429. As a further act of penitence, her head was shaved. When she adopted male dress and a warrior's harness, Joan had cut her hair "in the round" in the style later made famous by the title character of the *Prince Valiant* comic strip. Her mannish hair was considered as offensive as her clothes, so it was cropped off.[2] Ominously, her male attire was not taken away, merely put in a sack and left in her cell.

VICTIM OF A TRAP

Joan's confession and her resumption of female dress occurred on Thursday, May 24, 1431. For three days she kept to her cell. On Sunday morning, she asked her jailer to release her from her chains so she might go to the toilet. She had been sleeping in her clothes, but when she removed the outer dress one of the soldiers took it from her, then threw her forbidden male garments on the bed. The guard stuffed her dress in the sack and told Joan to do what she needed to do. When she was finished, she had nothing to put on but male clothing. Joan protested, saying she could not don men's clothing again. This is exactly what the English guards were trying to make her do, and they refused to return her dress. Some hours passed, and Joan had to go to the lavatory again. She had no choice, given her strong sense of modesty, but to put on the forbidden clothes.

When court official Friar Martin Ladvenu visited her, he found Joan distraught. He claimed later that Joan had told him she had been raped by an English lord, but no one else with access to Joan in prison corroborated this story. It's not impossible, just unproven.[3]

Word quickly reached Cauchon that his prisoner had broken her word and reverted to male dress. He went to Joan's cell on Monday, May 28 with his secretary,

Boisguillaume, and another assessor. Cauchon found Joan as reported, wearing a man's tunic, hood, and hose.[4] He asked her why she had lapsed so quickly into error.

Her answer was not witnessed by anyone who favored her. Boisguillaume recorded her as saying, "I took it of my own free will. No one constrained me to take it. I prefer to dress as a man than as a woman . . . I never understood that I had sworn not to resume it . . . I thought it more proper, being amongst men, than to dress as a woman."[5]

She then went on to say Cauchon had broken faith with her. He had said she could attend mass if she wore women's clothes, but she was never let out to do so. Cauchon promised to free her from her shackles, which she hated, and here she was still chained to a heavy timber. Joan offered to go to an ecclesiastical prison and wear female attire ever after, if Cauchon would simply live up to his word.

Having fallen into her enemies' trap, Joan saw no reason to die under false pretenses. To Cauchon's face she reiterated her belief in her voices, and their words, coming from God, were truer than anything mortal men could say—including any representative of the Church Militant.

Boisguillaume, writing all this down, scrawled two words in Latin in the margin by Joan's declaration: *Responsio mortifera*, meaning fatal answer.[6]

Cauchon left her, as his secretary noted, "to proceed further according to law and reason."

The bishop encountered the Earl of Warwick in the castle courtyard. Upon seeing him, Cauchon laughed and said, "Be of good cheer, it is done! We've got her!"[7]

Everything happened with speed. Cauchon promptly turned Joan over to the authorities of Rouen for punishment. A few of the court assessors urged she be given another chance to recant, but Cauchon dismissed their advice. Joan was now officially a relapsed heretic. The law would take its course. Her execution was scheduled for the next day, at eight o'clock in the morning.

Brother Ladvenu and Brother Toutmouille went to Joan to hear her confession. They found her weeping. The enormity of what was about to happen had overwhelmed her. She recovered a bit when Cauchon appeared.

"Bishop, I die through you," she said.

"Ah, Joan, be patient. You die because you did not keep your promise but returned to your former evil-doing," Cauchon replied.

She told him, "Alas! If you had put me in Church prisons and in the hands of competent and suitable Church guards, this would not have happened; that is why I appeal to God about you."[8]

Joan passed the night in despair. She had said at her trial she hoped to be rescued, but one of her voices told her to expect martyrdom. Once again they were right. To the last, she told Brother Ladvenu she believed her voices came from God, and they had not deceived her.[9]

Friar and trial usher Jean Massieu accompanied Joan to the executioner's cart. She was to be burned at a stake set up in Rouen's marketplace. A hundred English soldiers surrounded the small cart, armed with "riot gear": swords, axes, and sticks to beat off any mob that might attempt to interfere with the execution.[10] She wore a simple shift, and

Joan of Arc is led to the stake to be burned to death in this 1867 painting by Isidore Patrois.

heretic's cap was placed on her head. This was a paper hat with the words *Heretic, Relapsed, Apostate, Idolater* written on it for all to see.[11]

BURNED AT THE STAKE

Word spread quickly of the execution, and by the time Joan arrived in the square a crowd of ten thousand had massed there, plus another thousand English troops. There were three platforms in the square, one for the judges, one for the attending priests, and one for Joan. A sign on her platform declared, "Joan, called the Maid, liar, pernicious, seducer of the people, diviner, superstitious, blasphemer of God, presumptuous, misbelieving the faith of Jesus Christ, braggart, idolater, cruel, dissolute, invoker of devils, apostate, schismatic, and heretic."[12]

She was taken to the priests first. The platform was high enough so that the entire crowd could see her as she ascended the steps. After an address by the priest, Joan fell to her knees and prayed loudly, asking for mercy and begging God to forgive her enemies. She went on like this for half an hour, and her pleas were so moving even some of the English witnesses wept.[13]

Not everyone was touched. Annoyed with the French judges for allowing Joan to go on so long, one of the English captains complained loudly, "Priest, are you going to let us get done in time for dinner?"[14]

When she rose, Massieu gave her a small cross he had made from sticks. No one else thought to do her this small kindness. She clasped it to her chest. Then Cauchon pronounced final sentence on her. As a relapsed heretic, the Church excommunicated her, casting her out of any chance of salvation. The Bailiff of Rouen, whose job it was to enforce the law against ordinary criminals, waved a hand at Joan, saying, "Away with her."[15]

English soldiers dragged her to the platform on which she was to die. It was high and faced with plaster, the better to be seen by the crowd and withstand the heat of the fire. She was lashed to the stake with her heretic's cap on her head. The executioner, a man named Geoffroy Thérage, complained to the judges the high platform prevented him from doing his job correctly. Once the fire was going, he couldn't get near the stake. Often an executioner would finish off a suffering victim, out of pity. The English were having none of that.[16]

One of the court assessors, Isambard de la Pierre, fetched a crucifix from the nearby church of St. Laurent.[17] He climbed up to Joan and held it up for her to gaze upon. She warned him he would have to get down when the flames rose, but she asked de la Pierre to keep the crucifix in her sight.

Thérage lighted the bundles of dry wood heaped around Joan's feet. As the flames mounted, Joan cried out, "Rouen, Rouen, am I to die here?" then "Ah, Rouen, I fear you will suffer for my death!"[18]

Soon she could do nothing but cry "Jesus! Jesus!" over and over, and with her last breath cried again "Jesus!" Then she spoke no more.

Halfway through the burning, Thérage was ordered to draw aside the blazing wood so the crowd could see Joan was dead. There would be no legend she escaped the flames. Still hanging on the stake was the naked, charred body of Joan of Arc. It was a terrible sight, even for people used to public executions. When the French judges and English soldiers were satisfied, the wood was piled over the body so that the fire would consume her completely.

Many wept at the awful spectacle. John Tessart, secretary to King Henry VI of England, was heard to say, "We are lost! We have burned a saint!"[19] Others in the crowd were overcome with grief or terror of God's retribution. Even the executioner, presumably a hardened man, reported to his superiors he feared he was damned for burning a saint. God would never forgive him, he said.

After several hours, the fire burned out. By the order of the English Cardinal Beaufort, all that remained of Joan of Arc was thrown in the river Seine.[20]

FRANCE REMADE

THE HUNDRED YEARS WAR WENT ON WITHOUT
Joan. The Duke of Bedford wrote to Philip the Good of
Burgundy to let him know the "witch" had been disposed
of. Even though the church court dropped all charges of
witchcraft against Joan, the English persisted in attri-
buting her influence and her victories to sorcery. The
Burgundians took a more sophisticated view. They were
glad to be rid of Joan, but the problem she created—an
active patriotic movement, led by a legitimate king of
France, Charles VII—still remained.

With Joan dead, the Duke of Bedford moved to counter
her achievements. He had the nine-year-old Henry VI
brought to Paris to be crowned king of France in
December 1431. There was no hope of getting him to
Reims, strongly held by royalist forces. The boy king was
warmly welcomed in Paris. He was the son of a French
princess, and the grandson of King Charles VI. On
December 16, Henry VI was crowned in Notre Dame

cathedral. As a public-relations gesture, a great banquet was held. A large crowd flocked to the feast, but the food was stale and cold. The good will sought by Henry VI was squandered by bad cuisine.[1] Worse, none of the notables of Paris found it worthwhile to publicly support young Henry. They knew the coronation was a sham. The English reaped no benefit from it at all.

LAST DAYS OF THE HUNDRED YEARS WAR

Soon after Philip the Good served notice to his English allies he had come to a preliminary agreement with Charles VII. The war had not gone well for Burgundy, even with Joan in prison. Philip had to raise the siege of Compiègne in October 1430. Vigorous campaigns in Normandy by La Hire and John of Dunois demonstrated the Armagnac faction was not giving up just because their inspiration had been captured. Philip signed a truce with Charles VII the same month Henry VI was crowned. The period of peace was an exceptional six years, and Philip gave every sign of making the truce permanent.[2]

Charles VII always preferred diplomacy to war. It suited his nature, and it suited the preferences of his intimate adviser, Georges de la Tremoille. Tremoille's influence had grown great. His insistence on peace at almost any price became so pronounced that a plot was made to remove him from the king's court. Hard-liners who wanted to drive the English out decided to do something about Tremoille. The Constable of France, Arthur de Richemont, aided by Queen Marie of Anjou, Charles du Maine, and Queen Yolande of Sicily resolved to kill him.[3] The king's friend and adviser was stabbed in the stomach, but his fat belly saved him from a fatal wound. Tremoille took the hint and retired, never to return to the court of Charles VII. Thereafter, the war against the English resumed with new vigor.

Peace between Burgundy and France became permanent with the Treaty of Arras, signed on September 20, 1435. The Duke of Bedford died of illness six days before the treaty was signed. He passed away in Rouen castle, where Joan had been held prisoner four years earlier.[4]

Without Burgundian support, the small English army could not control the territory it held. The conquests of Henry V began to crumble. Normandy seethed with rebellion, which the English could not check. In April 1436, Arthur de Richemont took advantage of English weakness to march into Paris. The city speedily fell to him, fulfilling a prophecy by Joan that within seven years (of 1431) the English would lose the greatest prize they ever had in France. Cautious Charles waited nineteen months before he entered the chief city of his realm. When he did, "he was fêted like God himself."[5] Many Frenchmen who sided with Burgundy and England fled for their lives, including Pierre Cauchon. The bishop escaped, and he continued to serve the English for the rest of his life. He died in 1442 of an apparent heart attack while being shaved by his barber.[6]

Charles VII was now master of most of France. The only provinces still held by the English were Normandy in the north and Aquitaine in the south. They were targeted for liberation. With Joan's example always in their minds, the royal army was reorganized. Gone were the wild, intemperate knights who ruined themselves and their country by their recklessness at Crécy, Poitiers, and Agincourt. Joan had been fond of artillery, using it extensively to knock down English fortifications and bolster the firepower of her often small army. After 1440, artillery became the foundation of the French power, as the royal army built up a formidable collection of cannon. Not only were the English blasted out of their castles, cannon proved to be the answer to the longbow. No longer could the English shelter behind stakes and wagons, showering the French with arrows. Cannon balls outranged longbow arrows, and when the English tried their old Agincourt tactics against the new French army they were shot to pieces.[7]

Normandy and Guienne were reconquered for France by 1461. That same year Charles VII died, being remembered as "Charles the Well-Served" for his luck in finding able subordinates. He was also remembered as the ungrateful king who let Joan of Arc die without doing much to save her. His son and successor, Louis XI, would oversee the destruction of Burgundy by 1477. Forty-six years after Joan's death, the fragmented land she left behind had been united. Though the English held on to bits of French real estate for almost another century (the city of Calais, for example, until 1558), the Hundred Years

War is usually considered to have ended in 1453 with the loss of Normandy.

In England, Henry VI grew to manhood a weak king, beset with bouts of insanity not unlike those suffered by his French grandfather, Charles VI. The dynastic struggle in France between Armagnacs and Burgundians was mirrored in England between rival branches of the royal family, the House of York and the House of Lancaster. The English factions fought a civil war for thirty years, the War of the Roses. It ended when a nobleman, Henry Tudor, deposed King Richard III in 1485. The Plantagenet line of kings passed into history. Their longtime enemies, the House of Valois, survived their downfall by another century.

THE FATE OF JOAN'S MEN

Of Joan's comrades in arms, the Duke d'Alençon lived a long, troubled life. Imprisoned several times by Charles VII and his son, Louis XI, for political reasons, d'Alençon died in 1476. Upon d'Alençon's death, Louis XI added his title to the crown, ending the line of dukes.[8]

John of Dunois lived long enough to also run afoul of Louis XI. Dismissed from court, he nonetheless worked to reconcile the king with various hostile nobles. He died peacefully on November 23, 1468.[9]

Gilles de Rais was executed in 1440 for monstrous crimes, including the mass murder of children. What drove this patriotic warrior to become one of the most infamous serial killers in history is unknown. Like his former comrade the Maid, de Rais died at the stake. Unlike Joan, who was brutally burned alive, the wealthy, nobly born de Rais was granted the mercy of strangulation before his body was fed to the flames.[10]

Étienne de Vignolles, called La Hire, led a colorful, violent life to the end. Charles VII made him Captain-General of Normandy, where he caused the English no end of trouble. Captured, La Hire was languishing in prison when Joan was burned at Rouen. Though unaccountably stingy when the Maid of Orléans was captured, Charles VII paid part of La Hire's ransom to the Burgundians. Set free, La Hire took part in the campaign in the south, where he died of sickness at Montauban on January 11, 1442. He's still remembered for the irreverent prayer, "May you do for La Hire what you would like La Hire to do for you, if you were La Hire and La Hire were God."[11]

The once-despised Arthur de Richemont, Constable of France, worked long and hard after Joan's death to drive the English out of France. He helped negotiate the Treaty of Arras between France and Burgundy in 1435, and his dramatic capture of Paris on April 13, 1436, spelled the end of anti-Armagnac control of France's largest city. His army cleared Normandy of the enemy by 1450. De Richemont's artillery ended the domination of the English longbow at the battle of Formigny that same year. Besides his success as a general, de Richemont also cleared the country of ruthless mercenary bands and sent the high-strung French nobility home to sulk in their castles while the grim business of war was settled. De Richemont died the day after Christmas 1458 at the advanced age (for a fighting man) of sixty-five.[12]

A GROWING LEGACY

The importance of Joan of Arc grew with each passing year. At first, her legacy was mainly a patriotic legend. She reminded the French how to fight and aroused their natural courage and love of their country. With her example before them, the outcome of the Hundred Years War was inevitable. England was too small a nation to control France, once France threw off its internal divisions

A Joan of Arc statue showing her waving her standard as she charges into battle can be seen in the Place des Pyramides in Paris, France. The statue was sculpted by Emmanuel Frémiet in the late nineteenth century.

and overcame the shame of so many defeats. While many titled, important men sought accommodation with the invaders, or used the weakness of the royal government to amass power for themselves, Joan used a simple message to reverse seventy years of defeat: God loves the King of France, and the King of France needs every Frenchman to drive out the foreign invaders. For this she was betrayed and abandoned to the cold calculation of her country's enemies. Her death was made as humiliating and as agonizing as possible, to undermine her message and diminish her fame. Her enemies' plan backfired. Burning Joan of Arc at the stake ensured her message would never be forgotten.

The second legacy of the Maid was religious. Because she made amazing things happen, stories of miracles followed in her wake. But Joan's final fame had one more hurdle to overcome. Though dead, she had to stand trial one more time.

FROM SOLDIER TO SAINT

CHARLES VII ENTERED ROUEN IN 1449. THE town had recently been taken from the English by the army under John of Dunois, now known as Count Dunois. The minutes of Joan's trial fell into the king's hands for the first time. Charles had done little to save Joan, and for this he has been severely criticized. What his personal feelings were about the Maid are unknown, though an observer in June 1431 reported the king felt "very bitter sorrow" over Joan's death. Pope Pius II said Charles VII "grieved bitterly" for Joan, and the king's chamberlain told the story that his master felt "sad but helpless" to help the woman who made him king.[1]

Once he had the trial documents, Charles asked one of his advisers, Guillaume Bouillé, dean of Noyon Cathedral, to review them. The official inquiry began February 15, 1450. Charles's view of the trial was clear. He said the English had "wickedly and unjustly had her killed, with great cruelty."[2]

Bouillé called many participants from the 1431 trial to testify, including Jean Massieu, Jean Beaupère, and the monks who had gone with her to the scaffold, Brothers Ladvenu and de la Pierre.[3] Their testimony was consistent. Joan did not have a fair trial. Pierre Cauchon had flouted laws and procedures to get Joan in his hands, and he used illegal methods to convict and execute her as well. With Bouillé's findings in hand, Charles decided to clear Joan's name of heresy and restore her reputation. He could not do so himself. She was tried and convicted by the Church, and only the Church could exonerate her.

Charles appealed to the new pope, Nicholas V. The pope was gravely concerned about the advance of the Turks into Europe (Constantinople fell to them a year later, in 1453). He wanted to organize a united front of Christian rulers to resist the Muslim Turks, so he was in the mood to accommodate Charles VII. Nicholas V sent a papal legate, Guillaume d'Estouteville, to Rouen to look into Bouillé's findings. D'Estouteville joined forces with the new Inquisitor of France, Jean Bréhal, and together they convened a new court of inquiry into the matter of Joan of Arc.[4]

A New Investigation

The church investigation opened on May 2, 1452. D'Estouteville and Bréhal went over the testimony collected for Charles VII. They had leading legal scholars examine the 1431 court's procedures. There were many obvious irregularities. Joan was held in a military prison instead of a church jail; she had no legal defender or advocate; there were constant assaults on her privacy and decency, especially after her virginity was upheld; and the fact that once Cauchon convicted her of relapsed heresy, he handed her over for execution.[5] By law, only civil authorities could execute someone. It was therefore necessary for a convicted heretic to be turned over to non-Church authorities before any sentence was carried out. In his haste to see Joan burn, Cauchon skipped this important step by delivering Joan directly to the executioner. It was also recognized that as Bishop of Beauvais, he had no jurisdiction over Joan's activities outside his district.

A large number of witnesses were called to the new trial. Several of the assessors who sat in Cauchon's court testified to what they said and did. The record of the trial was shown to be substantially correct, but the procedures were biased, unfair, and ultimately illegal. Bréhal wrote up a summary of the case and submitted it to a panel of distinguished lawyers. They promptly found for Joan.[6]

A New Trial

Nothing more happened for two years. Only when Joan's family moved for a new trial to clear their daughter's name did things go forward again. Pope Calixtus III granted their request in June 1455. The Rehabilitation Trial, as it became known, was held in Notre Dame cathedral in Paris—ironically, the scene of Henry VI's futile coronation as king of France.[7]

Most of the men behind Joan's trial were dead and gone. Cauchon, Jean d'Estivet, Nicolas Midi (who preached a sermon to Joan on the scaffold before her death), and many more were already beyond justice. Jean Lemaistre, the second judge, had disappeared.[8] The new court was not out to punish the judges of the old, but to remove the taint of heresy from Joan of Arc's memory.

The proceedings opened with the reading of a petition by Joan's aged mother, Isabelle Romée, in which she described her daughter as "born in lawful marriage, to whom the sacraments of baptism and confirmation were given, and who was raised in the fear of God and respect for the tradition of the Church. . . . [Joan] never thought, conceived, or did anything contrary to the faith." Her terrible fate was entirely due to "enemies who had her arraigned in Church court, and despite her disavowals and appeals they condemned her in a damnable and wicked trial, and put her to death most cruelly by fire."[9]

When the trial got under way, it covered the same ground as Cauchon's investigation, with inquiries being held at different points in Joan's life, from Domrémy to Orléans and Paris. Much of what we know today about Joan's background and personal behavior comes from sworn statements made at the Rehabilitation Trial. People as different as the neighbors of the Darc family and the Duke d'Alençon gave testimony. The sworn statements were studied, and in July 1456, Archbishop of Reims Jean Jouvenel des Ursins, declared the 1431 verdict null and void. It was entirely the result of political pressure by the English, not proper findings under Church law.

The archbishop wrote, "We proclaim that Joan did not contract any taint of infamy and that she shall be and is washed clean of such."[10] A cross was erected in the old market square of Rouen in memory of Joan.

One aspect of Joan's life not investigated by the Rehabilitation Trial was the alleged miracles that occurred around her. The change of winds at Orléans that allowed the boats with provisions to reach the city was popularly considered a miracle. Her predictions of her own wounding (and death) were widely discussed and believed, and the revival of the dead baby long enough to be baptized were some of the stories told about Joan. Her execution produced a crop of wondrous anecdotes. An English soldier who had sworn to help burn the witch saw a white dove arise from the flames.[11] Geoffroy Thérage, the executioner, complained fearfully that Joan's heart would not burn, even though he fed the fire with sulfur and oil. Preservation of organs from flame was considered a sign of sanctity.[12] The judges at the Rehabilitation Trial kept clear of such matters. They had not convened to make Joan a saint.

Elsewhere in France, the vindication of the Maid of Orléans was treated as cause for public celebration. From that time on, Joan of Arc became ever more popular in her native land. People found in her, her life, and her deeds the great things they wanted to find. She was a peasant who made a king. She was a virtuous woman and a deeply spiritual Catholic. She was a patriot and a warrior who came "not to send Peace, but a sword."[13]

Things changed in France because of Joan, in addition to the great military deeds she accomplished. Her heresy trial and subsequent rehabilitation gravely weakened the Holy Inquisition in France. The Inquisition grew stronger in Spain and Italy, where heretics were executed well into the eighteenth century. Not so in France. Joan's martyrdom exposed the potential injustice of Church trials, and the Inquisition never regained its power or authority in France after 1456.[14]

A New Honor

As the tide of history rolled on, each new generation found new meaning in Joan. Whenever France was threatened by foreign foes, the image of Joan rose again to call Frenchmen to arms. Her appeal adapted to the times. As the centuries rolled by, she was seen as a Catholic knight fighting Protestant heresy. She was also called an early Protestant, making her spiritual connection directly with God, avoiding the priesthood. After the French Revolution of 1789, Joan was out of favor for a time. She was associated with the old royal regime, now overthrown, but the French people would not give her up. During World War II, when General Charles de Gaulle's Free French forces needed a symbol to signify their continuing defiance of Nazi Germany, they chose the Cross of Lorraine (a cross with two horizontal bars). It was a perfect allusion to the most famous patriot of Lorraine, Joan of Arc.

Joan's reputation continued to grow spiritually as well. During her lifetime and after, people experienced dreams

SAINTHOOD

The modern Catholic Church has set procedures for the elevation of worthy persons to sainthood. Before *canonization*, being declared a saint, the candidate must first go through the process of *beatification*, being found worthy of veneration.[15]

If the reputation of a candidate reaches a certain level, the candidate's name and career are recommended to the Vatican for investigation. An investigator is chosen, and he undertakes to interview or collect information on the person in question. If the candidate is long deceased, historical research is necessary. Local church authorities are employed to collect information on the subject's reputation for sanctity, reports of miracles associated with the candidate (including visions and dreams), and interviews with witnesses. If the candidate wrote anything, it must be examined for content. The results of these inquiries are sent to Rome to the Congregation of Rites by secure messenger.

The evidence is handed over to a cardinal appointed by the pope to handle the case. The cardinal, the original investigator, and other relevant Church officials examine the evidence. If the evidence is found to be sound, a recommendation is made to proceed with the case (or end it, if the evidence is wanting). If the Congregation of Rites finds in favor of the candidate, they forward a recommendation to the pope. At this stage the candidate is granted the title "Venerable."

The cycle is repeated several times, with investigations being evaluated by the Congregation of Rites again and again as more evidence is collected. If authenticated miracles can be attributed to the candidate, the cardinals report this to the pope. The pope then officiates at a Beatification rite in the Vatican Basilica. The candidate is now known as the Blessed, and public veneration is now allowed, but not required. If two or more miracles can be attributed to the Blessed candidate, this is discussed at three meetings of the congregation. The pope may then issue a Bull of Canonization that not only permits but commands public veneration of the candidate.

and visions of her, much as she saw Saint Michael, Saint Margaret, and Saint Catherine. So many of these accounts had accumulated by 1869 that the bishop of Orléans, Felix Dupanloup, started a movement to make Joan a saint.[16] The movement impressed Pope Leo XIII enough to open an investigation of the miracles and visions associated with Joan. In 1909, she was beatified, a preliminary step toward sainthood. Full canonization as Saint Joan did not occur until 1920, after France's terrible losses in World War I.

The elevation of Joan to sainthood had nothing to do with her military or political feats. She was canonized for her virtues, her spirituality, and the miracles associated with her. Oddly enough, in modern times two of her guiding lights, Saint Margaret and Saint Catherine, have been purged from the ranks of Catholic saints. Historical investigations have shown both women did not exist.[17]

This being the case, whose voices did Joan hear? Whose images did she see? There's no answer to be had now. Like generations of French people, we must look at Joan and see what we want to see. Beyond the aura of sanctity that now surrounds Saint Joan, we can still plainly see the real Joan of Arc: the sturdy farmer's daughter, serious and good-hearted, who tended the family's flock and went regularly to church. That she, of all people of her day, would leave her home and journey far away to fight in battles and make a king—that is remarkable enough. The honesty and strength of one young girl changed history.

CHRONOLOGY

1337—The Hundred Years War begins.

1340—Edward III invades France. English naval victory at Sluys.

1346—Edward III invades France again. English victory at Crécy on August 26.

1356—The Black Prince defeats King John II of France at Poitiers.

1407—Louis of Orléans is assassinated by Burgundians. Beginning of the Armagnac-Burgundy feud.

1412—Joan of Arc born in Domrémy, province of Lorraine.

1415—Henry V of England invades France and defeats the French at Agincourt.

1419—Duke John (the Fearless) is assassinated. Dauphin Charles is implicated.

1428—*May:* Joan goes to Robert de Baudricourt and reveals her mission to see the dauphin crowned king of France.
October: The siege of Orléans begins.

1429—*January:* Joan returns to Vaucouleurs to see Robert de Baudricourt.
February 12: The Battle of the Herrings.
March 8: Joan meets the dauphin at Chinon castle.
March 12: Joan is questioned in Poitiers by a panel of churchmen.

March 22: Joan writes her "Letter to the English," warning them to leave France.

April 21: Joan joins the royal army at Blois.

April 29: Joan arrives at Orléans.

May 4: Joan and her followers capture the fort at St. Loup.

May 7: Capture of the Tourelles. The siege is broken, and Joan is wounded.

June 12: The French capture Jargeau.

June 15: The French capture the Loire bridges at Meung.

June 17: Beaugency falls to Joan's army.

June 18: The French pursue and defeat the English at Patay.

June 29: The new French army begins the march to Reims to crown Charles king.

July 2: Auxerre falls to the dauphin.

July 5–9: The French army arrives at Troyes. When Joan openly prepares to storm the city, it surrenders.

July 17: The dauphin is crowned King Charles VII in Reims.

August: Joan demands the royal army move against English-held Paris.

August 28: Charles VII signs a truce with Burgundy without Joan's knowledge.

September 8–9: Joan attacks Paris. She is wounded, and the attack fails.

September 12: The royal army retreats to the Loire valley.

September 21: Charles VII disbands the army and sends Duke d'Alençon home.

October-November: Joan moves against the mercenary Perrinet Gressart but fails to capture his home base.

December 25: Joan returns to Jargeau. She finds out her family has been ennobled.

1430—*March:* Without the king's consent, Joan goes to Compiègne to help the city resist a Burgundian attack.

May 14: Joan and a small army of followers arrive at Compiègne.

May 16: Joan's thrust against Choisy is repulsed by the Burgundians.

May 22: Compiègne is surrounded and besieged by Burgundy.

May 23: Joan is captured by Burgundian troops fighting outside Compiègne.

November: After being moved around various fortresses as a prisoner of the Burgundian lord, John of Luxembourg, Joan is sold to the English.

1431—*January 9:* Joan's trial begins in Rouen.

February 21: Joan's first public examination.

March 27: The Trial in Ordinary begins in Rouen Castle.

May 9: Joan is threatened with torture if she does not recant.

May 19: The University of Paris faculty and the Court Assessors give their opinion that Joan is guilty of heresy.

May 24: Joan abjures (swears she will change) her heresy.

May 29: Forced back into men's clothing, Joan is condemned as a relapsed heretic and sentenced to death by fire.

May 30: Joan of Arc is burned in the old market square of Rouen.

1435—*September 20:* Peace between Burgundy and France became permanent with the Treaty of Arras.

1436—Paris falls to Arthur de Richemont, Constable of France.

1437—Charles VII enters Paris.

1442—France takes Gascony from the English.

1450—*April 15:* Battle of Formigny, where French artillery defeats the English longbow. Normandy is recaptured for France.

1452—First inquiry about the legality of Joan's trial.

1453—*July:* The Battle of Castillon. England is defeated. This is the official end of the Hundred Years War.

1455—*June 11:* Pope Calixtus III authorizes a tribunal to reopen Joan's heresy trial.
December 7–12: Joan's Rehabilitation Trial opens at Notre Dame cathedral, Paris.

1456—*July 7:* Joan is officially rehabilitated by the Catholic Church.

1909—Joan is beatified.

1920—*May 16:* Joan of Arc canonized as Saint Joan of Arc.

CHAPTER NOTES

CHAPTER 1. FATE OR BETRAYAL?

1. Deborah A. Fraioli, *Joan of Arc and the Hundred Years War* (Westport, Conn.: Greenwood Press, 2005), p. lxiii.

2. Régine Pernoud and Marie-Véronique Clin, *Joan of Arc: Her Story* (New York: St. Martin's Press, 1998), p. 231.

3. Ibid, pp, 231–232.

4. Ibid., p. 220.

5. Marina Warner, *Joan of Arc: The Image of Female Heroism* (New York: Alfred A. Knopf, 1981), pp. 96–97.

6. Pernoud and Clin, pp. 232–233.

7. Ibid, p. 190.

8. Warner, pp. 44–47.

9. Pernoud and Clin, p. 232.

10. Ibid.

11. Warner, p. 75.

12. Kelly DeVries, *Joan of Arc: A Military Leader* (Phoenix Mills, U.K.: Sutton Publishing Ltd., 1999), p. 50, 106.

13. Warner, p. 75.

CHAPTER 3. FROM DOMRÉMY TO DAUPHIN

1. Marina Warner, *Joan of Arc: The Image of Female Heroism* (New York: Alfred A. Knopf, 1981), p. 75

2. Charles Wayland Lightbody. *The Judgements of Joan.* (Cambridge, Mass.: Harvard University Press, 1961), p. 56.

3. Frances Gies. *Joan of Arc: The Legend and the Reality.* (New York: Harper & Row, 1981), p. 8.

4. Victoria Sackville-West, *Saint Joan of Arc,* (Garden City, N.Y.: Doubleday, Doran & Company, Inc., 1936), p. 29.

5. Régine Pernoud, *Joan of Arc: By Herself and Her Witnesses,* Trans. Edward Hyams. (New York: Stein and Day, 1982), p. 15–16.

6. Ibid., p. 20.

7. Ibid., pp. 21–22.

8. Sackville-West, p. 30.

9. Ibid., p. 52.

10. Marina Warner, *Joan of Arc: The Image of Female Heroism.* (New York: Alfred A. Knopf, 1981), p. 14.

11. Sackville-West, p. 4.

12. Gies, p. 23.

13. Ibid.

14. Pernoud, p. 31.

15. Ibid., p. 33.

16. Sackville-West, p. 73.

17. Deborah A. Fraioli, *Joan of Arc and the Hundred Years War* (Westport, Conn.: Greenwood Press, 2005), p. 60.

18. Ibid., p. 61

19. Lightbody, p. 145

20. Fraioli, p. 61.

21. Régine Pernoud and Marie-Véronique Clin, *Joan of Arc: Her Story,* Trans. by Jeremy duQuesnay Adams (New York: St. Martin's Press, 1998), pp. 167–168.

22. Sackville-West, p. 122.

23. Ibid., pp. 123–124.

CHAPTER 4. ORLÉANS

1. Régine Pernoud and Marie-Véronique Clin, *Joan of Arc: Her Story*, Trans. by Jeremy duQuesnay Adams (New York: St. Martin's Press, 1998), p. 172.
2. Deborah A. Fraioli, *Joan of Arc and the Hundred Years War* (Westport, Conn.: Greenwood Press, 2005), p. 61.
3. Pernoud and Clin, p. 172.
4. Kelly DeVries, *Joan of Arc: A Military Leader.* (Bath, U.K.: Sutton Publishing, 1999), p. 50.
5. Régine Pernoud, *Joan of Arc: By Herself and Her Witnesses*, Trans. Edward Hyams. (New York: Stein and Day, 1982), p. 62.
6. Ibid., pp. 51–52.
7. Ibid., p. 59.
8. Victoria Sackville-West, Saint *Joan of Arc*, (Garden City, N.Y.: Doubleday, Doran & Company, Inc., 1936), p. 141.
9. Pernoud and Clin, pp. 180–181.
10. DeVries, p. 65.
11. Pernoud and Clin, p. 188.
12. DeVries, p. 66–67.
13. Ibid., pp. 68–69.
14. Ibid., p. 74–75.
15. Ibid., p. 77.
16. Ibid.
17. Ibid., pp. 78–79.
18. Marina Warner, *Joan of Arc: The Image of Female Heroism.* (New York: Alfred A. Knopf, 1981), p. 66.
19. Sackville-West, p. 182.
20. Warner, p. 67.
21. DeVries, p. 86.

22. Ibid., p. 90.

CHAPTER 5. WINNING THE LOIRE

1. Kelly DeVries, *Joan of Arc: A Military Leader.* (Bath, U.K.: Sutton Publishing, 1999), p. 94.
2. Ibid.
3. Régine Pernoud and Marie-Véronique Clin, *Joan of Arc: Her Story*, Trans. by Jeremy duQuesnay Adams (New York: St. Martin's Press, 1998), p. 54.
4. Ibid., p. 55.
5. Victoria Sackville-West, *Saint Joan of Arc*, (Garden City, N.Y.: Doubleday, Doran & Company, Inc., 1936), p. 197.
6. Ibid., p. 201.
7. Ibid. p. 202.
8. DeVries, p. 99.
9. Ibid., p. 100.
10. Frances Gies. *Joan of Arc: The Legend and the Reality.* (New York: Harper & Row, 1981), p. 92.
11. Ibid.
12. Ibid., pp. 93–94.
13. Gies, p. 94.
14. DeVries, p. 106–107.
15. Sackville-West, p. 206.
16. Gies, p. 95.
17. Ibid.
18. Ibid.
19. DeVries, p. 114.
20. Gies, p. 97.
21. Ibid., p. 98.
22. Ibid.

23. DeVries, p. 119–120.

24. Gies, p. 99.

25. Ibid., p. 99–100.

26. Ibid., p. 100.

CHAPTER 6. FROM DAUPHIN TO DIVINE KING

1. Frances Gies. *Joan of Arc: The Legend and the Reality.* (New York: Harper & Row, 1981), p. 103.

2. Ibid.

3. Victoria Sackville-West, *Saint Joan of Arc,* (Garden City, N.Y.: Doubleday, Doran & Company, Inc., 1936), p. 216.

4. Gies, p. 104.

5. Ibid., p. 105.

6. Kelly DeVries, *Joan of Arc: A Military Leader.* (Bath, U.K.: Sutton Publishing, 1999), p. 127.

7. Gies, p. 106.

8. Sackville-West, p. 219.

9. Gies, p. 107.

10. DeVries, pp. 131–132.

11. Ibid., p. 132.

12. Ibid., p. 132.

13. Ibid., p. 133.

14. Régine Pernoud and Marie-Véronique Clin, *Joan of Arc: Her Story,* Trans. by Jeremy duQuesnay Adams (New York: St. Martin's Press, 1998), p. 190.

15. DeVries, p. 133.

16. Gies, p. 110.

17. Ibid.

18. Ibid., p. 111–112.

19. Régine Pernoud, *Joan of Arc: By Herself and Her Witnesses*, Trans. Edward Hyams. (New York: Stein and Day, 1982), p. 125.

CHAPTER 7. TRUST NOT IN PRINCES

1. Kelly DeVries, *Joan of Arc: A Military Leader.* (Bath, U.K.: Sutton Publishing, 1999), pp. 135–136.
2. Victoria Sackville-West, *Saint Joan of Arc,* (Garden City, N.Y.: Doubleday, Doran & Company, Inc., 1936), p. 225.
3. Kelly DeVries, *Joan of Arc: A Military Leader.* (Bath, U.K.: Sutton Publishing, 1999), p. 139.
4. Ibid., p. 140.
5. Sackville-West, p. 229.
6. DeVries, p. 142–143.
7. Ibid., p. 144.
8. Ibid., p. 144–145.
9. Régine Pernoud and Marie-Véronique Clin, *Joan of Arc: Her Story*, Trans. by Jeremy duQuesnay Adams (New York: St. Martin's Press, 1998), p. 170.
10. Ibid.
11. DeVries, p. 145.
12. Ibid.
13. Ibid., pp. 147–149.
14. Régine Pernoud, *Joan of Arc: By Herself and Her Witnesses*, Trans. Edward Hyams. (New York: Stein and Day, 1982), pp. 136–137.
15. DeVries. p. 151.
16. Ibid., p. 153.
17. Sackville-West, p. 236.
18. Ibid., p. 237.

19. DeVries, pp. 158–159.

20. Ibid., pp. 164–165.

21. Ibid., p. 165–166.

22. Pernoud and Clin, p. 82.

23. Ibid., p. 83.

24. Ibid.

25. DeVries, p. 168.

CHAPTER 8. SOLD TO THE HIGHEST BIDDER

1. Frances Gies. *Joan of Arc: The Legend and the Reality.* (New York: Harper & Row, 1981), p. 141.

2. Ibid., p. 142.

3. Ibid., p. 143.

4. Marina Warner, *Joan of Arc: The Image of Female Heroism.* (New York: Alfred A. Knopf, 1981), p. 75.

5. Victoria Sackville-West, *Saint Joan of Arc,* (Garden City, N.Y.: Doubleday, Doran & Company, Inc., 1936), p. 264.

6. Gies, p. 147.

7. Sackville-West, p. 266–267.

8. Ibid., p. 268–269.

9. Gies, p. 149.

10. Sackville-West, p.267.

11. Gies, p. 150.

12. Ibid.

CHAPTER 9. TRIAL AND ERRORS

1. Régine Pernoud and Marie-Véronique Clin, *Joan of Arc: Her Story,* Trans. by Jeremy duQuesnay Adams (New York: St. Martin's Press, 1998), p. 167.

2. Régine Pernoud, *Joan of Arc: By Herself and Her Witnesses*, Trans. Edward Hyams. (New York: Stein and Day, 1982), p. 161.

3. Pernoud and Clin, p. 104.

4. Frances Gies. *Joan of Arc: The Legend and the Reality.* (New York: Harper & Row, 1981), pp. 153–154.

5. Ibid.

6. Ibid.

7. Pernoud and Clin, pp. 208–209.

8. Pernoud and Clin, p. 105.

9. Victoria Sackville-West, *Saint Joan of Arc*, (Garden City, N.Y.: Doubleday, Doran & Company, Inc., 1936), p. 286.

10. Pernoud and Clin, p. 214.

11. Pernoud, p. 165.

12. Pernoud and Clin, p. 272.

13. W. P. Barrett, trans., *The Trial of Jeanne d'Arc.* (London: George Routledge & Sons, Lts., 1931), p. 45.

14. Ibid., p. 50.

15. Ibid.

16. Ibid., p. 51.

17. Pernoud and Clin, p. 207.

18. Monica Furlong, ed., *The Trial of Joan of Arc.* (Evesham, UK: Arthur James, 1996), p. 48.

19. Ibid., p. 49.

20. Barrett, p. 57.

21. Ibid., p. 58.

22. Ibid., p. 69.

23. Pernoud and Clin, p. 116.

24. Gies, p. 160.

25. Rossell Hope Robbins, *The Encyclopedia of Witchcraft and Demonology* (New York: Crown Publishers, 1959), p. 285.

26. Ibid.

27. Barrett, p. 70.

28. Robbins, p. 285.

29. Gies, p. 202.

30. Ibid.

31. Ibid., p. 203.

32. Robbins, p. 285.

33. Ibid.

34. Pernoud and Clin, p. 233.

35. Gies, p. 214.

36. Sackville-West, p. 331.

CHAPTER 10. CONSIGNED TO FLAME

1. Victoria Sackville-West, *Saint Joan of Arc* (Garden City, N.Y.: Doubleday, Doran & Company, Inc., 1936), p. 331.

2. Ibid., p. 332.

3. Frances Gies. *Joan of Arc: The Legend and the Reality*. (New York: Harper & Row, 1981), p. 216.

4. Ibid., p. 217.

5. Sackville-West, p. 335.

6. Gies,.p. 217.

7. Ibid., p. 218.

8. Dialogue reproduced in Gies, p. 220.

9. Ibid., p, 221.

10. Sackville-West, p. 338.

11. Gies, p. 222.

12. Ibid.

13. Sackville-West, p. 339.

14. Pernoud and Clin, p. 135.

15. Sackville-West, p. 340.

16. Gies, p. 224.

17. Pernoud and Clin, p. 136.

18. Gies, p. 224.

19. Sackville-West, p. 340.

20. Gies, p. 224.

CHAPTER 11. FRANCE REMADE

1. Frances Gies, *Joan of Arc: The Legend and the Reality.* (New York: Harper & Row, 1981), p. 227.

2. Pernoud, p. 256.

3. Ibid.

4. Régine Pernoud and Marie-Véronique Clin, *Joan of Arc: Her Story,* Trans. by Jeremy duQuesnay Adams (New York: St. Martin's Press, 1998), p. 176.

5. Régine Pernoud, *Joan of Arc: By Herself and Her Witnesses,* Trans. Edward Hyams. (New York: Stein and Day, 1982), pp. 256–257.

6. Pernoud and Clin, p. 210.

7. Terence Wise, *Medieval Warfare,* (New York: Hastings House Publishers, 1976), pp. 119–120.

8. Pernoud and Clin, p. 173.

9. Ibid., p. 181.

10. Ibid., p. 198.

11. Ibid., p. 188.

12. Ibid., p. 199.

CHAPTER 12. FROM SOLDIER TO SAINT

1. Frances Gies, *Joan of Arc: The Legend and the Reality.* (New York: Harper & Row, 1981), p. 231.

2. Ibid., p. 231–232.

3. Régine Pernoud, *Joan of Arc: By Herself and Her Witnesses,* Trans. Edward Hyams. (New York: Stein and Day, 1982), p. 259.

4. Ibid., pp. 260–261.

5. Ibid., p. 261.

6. Gies, p. 235.

7. Charles Wayland Lightbody. *The Judgements of Joan.* (Cambridge, Mass.: Harvard University Press, 1961), p. 124.

8. Gies, p. 235.

9. Ibid.

10. Pernoud, p. 269.

11. Ibid., p. 233.

12. Gies, p. 225.

13. King James Bible: Matthew 10, verse 34.

14. Lightbody, pp. 124–125.

15. "Canonization," *The New Catholic Encyclopedia Online,* n.d., <http://www.newadvent.org/cathen/02364b.htm> (January 24, 2007).

16. Gies, pp. 238–239.

17. Ibid., p. 239.

Glossary

Armagnac—A French noble family, associated with the royalist cause loyal to the kings of France.

assessor—A scholar of church law. Up to sixty assessors attended the trail of Joan of Arc, recording the procedure and posing questions to her.

bastion—A small fortified position, often part of a larger fortress.

beatification—A process used by the Catholic Church to identify persons of unusual spiritual gifts. A beatified person earns the title "Blessed." Usually beatification is a prelude to canonization, the process of becoming a saint.

Black Death—Also known as the bubonic plague. This disease swept through Europe in the mid-fourteenth century, killing an estimated one third of the population.

Black Prince—Edward, Prince of Wales, son of King Edward III of England. He lived from 1330–1376.

Burgundy—A province in eastern France ruled by dukes during the Hundred Years War.

canonization—The process by which the Catholic Church designates someone a saint.

Capetian—The dynasty of French kings descended from Hugh Capet, lasting from A.D. 987 to A.D. 1328.

Church Militant—The entire membership of the Catholic Church on Earth.

Church Triumphant—God, Christ, angels, saints, and the souls of Catholics in Heaven make up the Church Triumphant.

coronation—The ceremony in which a king is crowned. In many countries, a king is not truly king until he has undergone his coronation.

crusade—Wars organized by the Catholic Church with the aim of conquering the Holy Land, then controlled by Muslim Arabs or Turks.

dauphin—Literally "dolphin," the title used by the eldest son of the king of France from 1349 until 1830. The dauphin was the heir apparent to the French throne, just as the Prince of Wales was the heir to the English throne.

duchy—A domain ruled by a duke or duchess.

Flanders—A province in northwest Europe, corresponding to modern Belgium. During the Hundred Years War, Flanders belonged to France but sided with England.

heresy—Ideas or doctrines contrary to the standard doctrine.

Inquisition—An organization within the Catholic Church charged with suppressing heresy. An investigator for the Inquisition is called an inquisitor.

longbow—English weapon, a wooden bow about six feet long. A longbow could launch an arrow up to four hundred yards at a rate of about ten to twelve per minute.

monarchy—The system of government in which a king or queen rules the nation.

Normandy—Northern province of France, facing England across the Channel.

Plantagenet—Dynasty of English kings who ruled from 1154 to 1485.

prelate—A churchman of high rank.

Saracen—European name for Muslim Arabs during the Middle Ages.

succession—The method by which one ruler follows another. In medieval Europe, the oldest son usually succeeded to the titles and possessions of his deceased father. Rules of succession were spelled out in great detail to prevent fighting over who would follow a dead king, but ambitious candidates fought anyway.

Valois—Dynasty of French kings who ruled from 1328 to 1589.

FURTHER READING

Bull, Angela. *Joan of Arc*. New York: Dorling Kindersley Pub., 2000

Burne, Alfred H. *The Hundred Years' War*. London: Penguin, 2002

Hilliam, David. *Joan of Arc: Heroine of France*. New York: Rosen Pub. Group, 2005.

Pickels, Dwayne E. *Joan of Arc*. Philadelphia: Chelsea House Publishers, 2002.

Roberts, Jeremy. Saint *Joan of Arc*. Minneapolis: Lerner Publicatons Co., 2000.

Silverthorne, Elizabeth. *Joan of Arc*. Detroit: Lucent Books, 2005.

Whiting, Jim. *The Life and Times of Joan of Arc*. Hockessin, Del.: Mitchell Lane Publishers, 2006.

INTERNET ADDRESSES

THE COUNTRY OF JOAN OF ARC

A guide to the district where Joan lived, including maps and photos.

   <http://www.stjoan-center.com/meuse/>

JOAN OF ARC QUIZ

In "search" box, type "Joan of Arc Quiz." Click on "Joan of Arc Quiz" at the top of the search results.

   <http://www.familyeducation.com>

SAINT JOAN OF ARC CENTER

   <http://www.stjoan-center.com/>

INDEX

HBRAX   +
        B
        J62T

THOMPSON, PAUL B.
    JOAN OF ARC

BRACEWELL
11/09